Editor
Erica N. Russikoff, M.A.

Editor in Chief
Karen J. Goldfluss, M.S. Ed.

Illustrator
Clint McKnight

Cover Artist
Brenda DiAntonis
Marilyn Goldberg

Art Coordinator
Renée Mc Elwee

Imaging
James Edward Grace
Craig Gunnell

Publisher

Mary D. Smith, M.S. Ed.

Spotlight On
AMERICA

African Americans

"America is a land of big dreamers and big hopes...And it is because our dreamers dreamed that we have emerged from each challenge more united, more prosperous, and more admired than before."

TCR 3395

Ida Bell Wells

Rosa Parks

Frederick Douglass

Teacher Created Resources

Author

Robert W. Smith

Teacher Created Resources
6421 Industry Way
Westminster, CA 92683
www.teachercreated.com
ISBN: 978-1-4206-3395-5

© *2011 Teacher Created Resources*
Made in U.S.A.

Teacher Created Resources

Table of Contents

Introduction

The *Spotlight on America* series is designed to introduce some of the seminal events in U.S. history to students in the fifth through eighth grades. Reading in the content area is enriched with a balanced variety of activities in written language, literature, social studies, and oral expression. The series is designed to make history come alive in your classroom and take root in the minds of your students.

African American History

The early history of the United States is inextricably linked with slavery. Africans were purchased in West Africa by slave traders and sold in the British colonies as slaves. The desire for freedom and the efforts to achieve freedom on the part of these slaves is an underlying current in the flow of American history, which reached a turning point with the Northern victory in the Civil War.

For African Americans, the dream of freedom was crushed under the weight of black codes, Jim Crow laws, and mob violence. Despite all of these overwhelming forces, African American individuals managed to achieve remarkable accomplishments in many facets of American life. Three concepts highlight the efforts of African Americans in the ninety years after the Civil War: the effort to attain education, the drive for economic success, and the desire for political and social equality. The rise of the civil rights movement from 1945 to 1970 under the determined leadership of many men and women finally offered African Americans an opportunity to participate in the political and economic life of the nation, while securing opportunities for education and advancement.

Reading Comprehension

The reading selections and comprehension questions in this book serve to introduce some of the most interesting and important African Americans in our history and the historical events that impacted their lives—from the settling of the colonies to the success of the civil rights movement.

Learning Activities

The readings in this book set the stage for activities in other subject areas. The literature readings are intended to bring students into the lives of these exceptional African American leaders and heroes and the events that so affected their lives. The activities in written language, public speaking, poetry, biography, and research are designed to help students recognize and empathize with these remarkable African Americans. The dramatic opportunities in Readers' Theater and Become a Famous Person impersonations will help all students walk in the footsteps of these courageous men and women. The activities with timelines, maps, and other social studies projects provide students with a sense of time, place, and historical perspective, while the culminating activities aim to give students a sense of living history. Enjoy using this book with your students, and look for other books in this series.

Teacher Lesson Plans
for Reading Comprehension

African Americans in Early America

Objective: Students will demonstrate fluency and comprehension in reading historically based text.

Materials: copies of African Americans in Early America (pages 7–11) and African Americans in Early America Quiz (page 36); additional reading selections from books, encyclopedias, and Internet sources for enrichment

Procedure

1. Reproduce and distribute the African Americans in Early America reading selection. Review pre-reading skills by briefly reviewing text and encouraging students to underline, make notes in the margins, write questions, and highlight unfamiliar words as they read.

2. Have students read the selection independently, in small groups, or together as a class.

3. As a class, discuss the following questions (or others of your choosing):

   • Who was the most interesting African American? Why?

   • How did the institution of slavery harm America? Explain your position using facts from the reading.

   • If you were a slave on the "Middle Passage," what would you do? Explain your answer.

Assessment: Have students complete the African Americans in Early America Quiz and underline the sentences in the reading selection where the answers were found. Correct the quizzes together.

Leaders Before the Civil War

Objective: Students will demonstrate fluency and comprehension in reading historically based text.

Materials: copies of Leaders Before the Civil War (pages 12–16) and Leaders Before the Civil War Quiz (page 37); additional reading selections from books, encyclopedias, and Internet sources for enrichment

Procedure

1. Reproduce and distribute the Leaders Before the Civil War reading selection. Review pre-reading skills by briefly reviewing text and encouraging students to underline, make notes in the margins, write questions, and highlight unfamiliar words as they read.

2. Have students read the selection independently, in small groups, or together as a class.

3. As a class, discuss the following questions (or others of your choosing):

   • Which African American leader do you admire most? Why?

   • Which leader was the most important? Explain your choice.

   • Which leader would you most like to interview? Why?

Assessment: Have students complete the Leaders Before the Civil War Quiz and underline the sentences in the reading selection where the answers were found. Correct the quizzes together.

Teacher Lesson Plans
for Reading Comprehension *(cont.)*

War, Reconstruction, and Segregation

Objective: Students will demonstrate fluency and comprehension in reading historically based text.

Materials: copies of War, Reconstruction, and Segregation (pages 17–20) and War, Reconstruction, and Segregation Quiz (page 38); additional reading selections from books, encyclopedias, and Internet sources for enrichment

Procedure

1. Reproduce and distribute the War, Reconstruction, and Segregation reading selection. Review pre-reading skills by briefly reviewing text and encouraging students to underline, make notes in the margins, write questions, and highlight unfamiliar words as they read.

2. Have students read the selection independently, in small groups, or together as a class.

3. As a class, discuss the following questions (or others of your choosing):
   - Was Reconstruction a failure? Explain your answer.
   - Which actions by white Southerners were most effective in segregating African Americans? Explain your position using facts from the reading.
   - How did African Americans succeed despite segregation? Explain your answer.

Assessment: Have students complete the War, Reconstruction, and Segregation Quiz and underline the sentences in the reading selection where the answers were found. Correct the quizzes together.

Leaders and Heroes

Objective: Students will demonstrate fluency and comprehension in reading historically based text.

Materials: copies of Leaders from the Civil War to the Great Depression (pages 21–24) and Leaders from the Civil War to the Great Depression Quiz (page 39); copies of African American Heroes, 1865–1940 (pages 25–28) and African American Heroes, 1865–1940 Quiz (page 40); additional reading selections from books, encyclopedias, and Internet sources for enrichment

Procedure

1. Reproduce and distribute the Leaders from the Civil War to the Great Depression and the African American Heroes, 1865–1940 reading selections. Review pre-reading skills by briefly reviewing text and encouraging students to underline, make notes in the margins, write questions, and highlight unfamiliar words as they read.

2. Have students read the selections independently, in small groups, or together as a class.

3. As a class, discuss the following questions (or others of your choosing):
   - Which leader did you most agree with? Explain your choice.
   - Which leader was most effective in helping African Americans? Explain your answer.
   - Which leader or hero would you like to know personally? Why?

Assessment: Have students complete the Leaders from the Civil War to the Great Depression Quiz and African American Heroes, 1865–1940 Quiz, and underline the sentences in the reading selection where the answers were found. Correct the quizzes together.

Teacher Lesson Plans for Reading Comprehension *(cont.)*

The Civil Rights Movement, 1945–1970

Objective: Students will demonstrate fluency and comprehension in reading historically based text.

Materials: copies of The Civil Rights Movement, 1945–1970 (pages 29–31) and The Civil Rights Movement, 1945–1970 Quiz (page 41); additional reading selections from books, encyclopedias, and Internet sources for enrichment

Procedure

1. Reproduce and distribute The Civil Rights Movement, 1945–1970 reading selection. Review pre-reading skills by briefly reviewing text and encouraging students to underline, make notes in the margins, write questions, and highlight unfamiliar words as they read.

2. Have students read the selection independently, in small groups, or together as a class.

3. As a class, discuss the following questions (or others of your choosing):

   • What was the importance of Emmett Till's murder?

   • What was the immediate effect of the *Brown* decision?

   • How did television affect the civil rights movement?

Assessment: Have students complete The Civil Rights Movement, 1945–1970 Quiz and underline the sentences in the reading selection where the answers were found. Correct the quizzes together.

Moments and Movers in the Civil Rights Movement

Objective: Students will demonstrate fluency and comprehension in reading historically based text.

Materials: copies of Moments and Movers in the Civil Rights Movement (pages 32–35) and Moments and Movers in the Civil Rights Movement Quiz (page 42); additional reading selections from books, encyclopedias, and Internet sources for enrichment

Procedure

1. Reproduce and distribute the Moments and Movers in the Civil Rights Movement reading selection. Review pre-reading skills by briefly reviewing text and encouraging students to underline, make notes in the margins, write questions, and highlight unfamiliar words as they read.

2. Have students read the selection independently, in small groups, or together as a class.

3. As a class, discuss the following questions (or others of your choosing):

   • Which group or person in the movement showed the most courage? Explain your answer.

   • Which leader faced the greatest challenge? Explain your choice.

   • Which person would you like to know or talk to? Why?

Assessment: Have students complete the Moments and Movers in the Civil Rights Movement Quiz and underline the sentences in the reading selection where the answers were found. Correct the quizzes together.

 Reading Passages

African Americans in Early America

The Roots of Slavery

The first Africans brought to Jamestown, Virginia, in the early 1600s were treated as indentured servants (like whites from debtor's prisons). However, a system of buying Africans and employing them as slaves soon developed. Most slaves came from West Africa, where they had been captured in tribal warfare or kidnapped for sale. Arab and European slave traders purchased these slaves with rum, cloth, tobacco, and guns, which were greatly prized by the contending tribes. Africans had captured and sold slaves as part of their tribal warfare since ancient times.

The Middle Passage

Most slaves had seen their families killed and villages destroyed. Slaves were marched to the western coast of Africa where they were taken on ships that traveled to the American colonies. This "Middle Passage" aboard slave ships was particularly savage because slaves were usually chained tightly together below decks for twenty-three hours a day.

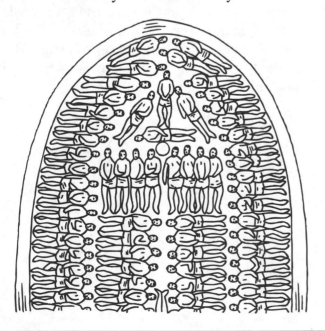

Slavery Before the Civil War

Newly arrived slaves in America were sold to plantation owners and farmers in the South and to merchants, farmers, and families in the North. Slavery was not as profitable in the North; large plantations and cash crops, such as cotton, rice, and tobacco, were far more common in the South. By 1800, many northern states had passed laws leading to the gradual end of slavery. Thousands of free African Americans worked on ships, in factories, or as laborers on farms. They did not receive equal treatment and were usually excluded from schools and churches, but they were not anybody's property. By 1860, there were about half a million free African Americans in the United States, most of them residing in the North.

Free African Americans, slaves who escaped from the South, and recently emancipated slaves in the North became a vocal minority opposed to the institution of slavery. They told of their experiences in publications and public meetings. Some prominent leaders, such as Benjamin Franklin and John Quincy Adams, became strong opponents of slavery.

Reading
Passages

African Americans in Early America *(cont.)*

Slavery in the South

The invention of the cotton gin in 1793 made raising cotton extremely profitable for plantation owners in the South, but this business was based on cheap slave labor. The South became more dependent upon slavery and more defensive about it as Northern abolitionists—led by ministers, Quakers, some politicians, and free African Americans— campaigned against slavery and its evils and developed an Underground Railroad to help slaves escape. There were about four million slaves in the South by 1860.

Plantation slaves were often treated with great cruelty. White owners became fearful of organized rebellion, such as the Nat Turner revolt. Legal restraints and Southern culture forbade the teaching of slaves to read or write; controlled their personal and family lives; and often used extreme violence to punish any suspicion of rebellion, escape, or independent behavior.

Compromise

The deepening divisions over slavery led to two major political compromises. The Missouri Compromise of 1820 allowed two new states—Missouri and Maine—to enter the Union with Missouri as a slave state and Maine as a free state. This kept a balance of power of twelve slave states and twelve free states. The Compromise of 1850 allowed residents in new states, such as California, Nevada, and other states obtained in the Mexican War, to decide for themselves whether to accept slavery in each state.

Congress also passed a very strict new Fugitive Slave Law that required Northern officials to help capture and return escaped slaves. This law made it necessary for fugitive slaves to escape to Canada in order to be free. The law infuriated Northern abolitionists, as well as other leaders in the states, and led to increased opposition to slavery.

The publication of *Uncle Tom's Cabin* by Harriet Beecher Stowe in 1852 led to deep antagonism among many citizens in the North to the idea of slavery as an institution. The author used the true experiences of escaped slaves to create a novel that portrayed slavery in all of its viciousness and evil.

Reading
Passages

African Americans in Early America *(cont.)*

A few of the many interesting individuals of African descent who lived during the colonial years are described below.

Esteban the Black, Explorer

Esteban the Black was a slave captured in Northern Africa, brought to Spain, and owned by a Spanish explorer named Andrés Dorantes. He accompanied Dorantes on an expedition to Florida in 1528. Esteban went ashore with Dorantes and about 300 men to explore the area near what is now Tampa Bay. They encountered unfriendly American Indians and fought repeatedly with many tribes while trying to find gold and later just trying to survive. Most of the men died from fever, disease, combat with the native people, or attacks from dangerous native animals.

The survivors were unable to find the ships that were supposed to wait for them. The remaining explorers built five small boats and tried to sail for Spanish settlements in the Caribbean, but they went the wrong way. They sailed along the coast of what is now Florida, Georgia, Alabama, Mississippi, and Louisiana. Three ships were wrecked by violent storms, and the remaining two crashed along the coast of Texas near Galveston Island. Esteban, Dorantes, and several of the men survived the crash and were captured by an American Indian tribe.

Four of the explorers were alive after five years of captivity, hunger, and very hard labor: Esteban, Dorantes, Cabeza de Vaca, and Maldonado. In 1534, they escaped from their captors and began a long journey in which they walked across Texas to the Pacific Coast and then down the coast of what is now Mexico.

Esteban got along well with the native tribes. He quickly learned native ways and made friends easily with these natives who had never seen an African American man before. Esteban also acquired a reputation as a healer.

When they arrived in Mexico City ten years after their journey began in Florida, the men were greeted as long-lost heroes. Despite the many times Esteban saved his life during the journey, Dorantes sold Esteban to the governor of Mexico. Because of his experience in exploring Texas and Mexico, Esteban was sent to guide an expedition into what is now the southwest United States in search of the legendary "Seven Cities of Gold" that were supposed to exist among some American Indian tribes. Esteban died on the journey to find these nonexistent golden cities.

Reading Passages

African Americans in Early America *(cont.)*

Jean Baptiste Pointe DuSable, Explorer

Jean DuSable was born in Haiti, the son of an African American slave and a white French sea captain. After his mother's death, his father had him educated in France, where he learned French, Spanish, and English. He worked as a sailor for his father until he was twenty. Then he and Jacques Clemorgan, an African American friend, sailed for America. They were shipwrecked along the coast of Louisiana near New Orleans. Afraid of being captured as runaway slaves, they quickly left New Orleans and traveled up the Mississippi River by boat. They trapped animals and traded furs along the way. Soon, they settled in St. Louis, Missouri, and set up a fur-trading business.

DuSable moved on to Fort Peoria, Illinois, and set up another fur-trading business. He met and married an American Indian girl who belonged to the Potawatomi tribe. DuSable made many trips to Canada to trap and trade furs, often stopping at a place American Indians called Eschikago. In 1779, he built a trading post for traveling fur trappers and brought his wife and many of her relatives to live in Eschikago.

The settlement grew and many people stopped to do business. In 1800, he sold the settlement and his business for $12,000 (a great deal of money at the time). The man who registered the sale in his own name got credit as the founder of Chicago until 1968 when DuSable was officially recognized as the city's founder.

Phillis Wheatley, Poet

An eight-year-old captured slave girl in Senegal, which is on the west coast of Africa, endured the treacherous "Middle Passage." The journey was made even worse by the cruelty of many of the ship's crew and the deaths of many slaves due to illness, starvation, and mistreatment. Thin, frail, ill, and wearing only rags, the girl was named for the ship, *Phillis*, that brought her to Boston. She was purchased by Susannah Wheatley, wife of a wealthy tailor, who gave her a surname. The family recognized the young slave girl's hunger for knowledge, and she soon was reading and studying with their eighteen-year-old daughter, who was also sickly. Within a year, Phillis had learned English, was reading the Bible, and was starting to learn Latin and Greek.

Reading Passages

African Americans in Early America *(cont.)*

Phillis Wheatley, Poet *(cont.)*

At the age of twelve, Phillis began to write poetry, and her first poem was published in 1770. She began to read her poetry to Boston leaders, including John Hancock. In 1773, she accompanied her owner's older son, Nathaniel Wheatley, to London where her first volume of poetry was published because no American printer would publish a work by a slave girl. In London, Phillis met many important dignitaries, including Benjamin Franklin.

After her return from England, she was emancipated by her owners. She wrote poetry before and during the American Revolution, eventually writing five books of poetry. Phillis even wrote to and met General Washington. Phillis married a freed slave and had three children, all of whom died in infancy. Her husband was often in debtor's prison. Phillis died at about the age of thirty—alone, unable to find a publisher for her latest poems, and destitute.

Benjamin Banneker, Inventor

Benjamin Banneker was the grandchild of a female white indentured servant (who earned her freedom after seven years) and an African American slave she bought and freed. Benjamin was born in 1731 in Maryland and grew up on a farm owned by his parents. His father adapted techniques of irrigation that he remembered from Africa. The channels and dams he dug made his farm very productive, and he helped neighbors learn effective methods of irrigation, too.

Benjamin had an opportunity to attend a private neighborhood boys' school. He was the only African American child at the school. He had already been taught to read by his parents and was very good in math. As Benjamin grew older, he designed clocks, studied astronomy, and learned to survey land. He published an almanac in the 1790s and worked as a surveyor who helped design the new city of Washington, D.C.

Other Important Individuals

These are a few of the many African Americans who made important contributions to life in the first centuries of development in North America. Other names include American patriot Crispus Attucks and Haitian rebel leader Toussaint L'Ouverture.

Reading Passages

Leaders Before the Civil War

The African Americans on these pages sometimes achieved success, while surviving terrible tragedies and enduring great hardships.

James P. Beckwourth, Mountain Man

James Pierce Beckwourth was the son of a white slave owner and an African American slave in Virginia in 1798. His father later moved to St. Louis, Missouri, which was on the edge of the unexplored western frontier. Jim's father sent him to live and work with a white blacksmith when he was fourteen years old. He became good at this trade, but he and the blacksmith had an argument over his late hours when Jim was courting a slave girl. Jim hit the blacksmith and ran away knowing he could be whipped or killed for hitting a white man.

Beckwourth wandered the frontier and worked as a salt miner for a while. Later, he joined a fur-trapping expedition led by General William Henry Ashley. Jim became a fur trapper and mountain man, as well as an explorer. He traveled to New Mexico, Arizona, California, and Mexico, as well as other western areas. Beckwourth discovered a path across the Sierra Nevada Mountains to the Long Valley in eastern California. He led the first wagon train through this path called "Beckwourth's Pass," which was later used by many western travelers and the Western Pacific Railroad. For a while, he ran a hotel and trading post near the pass.

Jim Beckwourth lived for many years with the Crow Indians and fought with them against their enemies, the Blackfoot and Cheyenne. He had several American Indian wives and became an important chief and tribal advisor. He was a very successful fur trapper who tried to steer the energies of the Crow people into trapping and trading rather than constant warfare. He eventually left the tribe to wander some more. In 1866, the United States Army asked him to help them make peace with the Crow Indians. They wanted him to return as their chief. He was killed, possibly by poisoning, during his efforts to negotiate a peace treaty.

Reading Passages

Leaders Before the Civil War *(cont.)*

Nat Turner, Rebel Against Slavery

Nat Turner was born in about 1800 to a slave named Nancy, who had been brought to America along the "Middle Passage" and sold to a plantation owner named Benjamin Turner. Little is known about Nat's father other than he ran away from the plantation when Nat was a child and was never heard from again. Although African Americans were taught to believe they were inferior, Nat was convinced by his mother and other slaves that he would grow up to be a prophet because of certain birthmarks on his body and because of his behavior and intelligence. Nat learned to read without anybody teaching him and despite the strict slave codes that forbade slaves to read or even to be taught to read.

Nat became a preacher in religious slave gatherings, and he was soon regarded as a prophet. Nat became convinced that he was chosen by God to lead a rebellion of slaves against their masters. He believed an eclipse of the sun in February 1831 was a sign that he should prepare to lead the revolt. Nat first aimed for July 4, 1831, as the day of liberation, but two earlier slave revolts led by others had failed, and Nat waited until the omens seemed right in August.

With several determined followers, Nat first attacked his owner, Joseph Travis, and the owner's entire family. Starting with a small team of six other slaves, Nat and his men went from plantation to plantation rousing the slaves to action. Nat's army of rebellion grew to more than sixty slaves who followed him into battle. They defeated a group of eighteen armed white men.

Soon, white slave owners realized a rebellion was going on, and Nat's slave army with few weapons and little discipline was under attack by as many as 3,000 armed white slave owners and state militia. Most of the slaves were captured and jailed. Many were severely punished. Nat Turner hid from his enemies in the woods for six weeks before he was captured and put in jail. His white attorney wrote a book telling Nat's story based on his interviews with Turner. It was called *The Confessions of Nat Turner,* in which Nat blamed the rebellion on the institution of slavery and his call as a prophet to end slavery. Nat Turner was sentenced to hang on November 11, 1831. His last words were: "I am ready."

Reading Passages

Leaders Before the Civil War *(cont.)*

Frederick Douglass, Abolitionist

Frederick Douglass was born a slave in 1818. He believed he was the son of a slave woman and her white owner. He was raised by his grandmother and then given to a family living in Baltimore. Here, he was given better clothes and food, as well as the supplies to learn how to read.

Eventually, he was sent to a plantation where he worked in the fields as a common slave. He was often beaten and left hungry by a brutal overseer. After a few years of mistreatment, he escaped to the North.

Douglass became a dynamic speaker at abolitionist meetings. He also wrote books about his life and experiences. He started several newspapers, which advocated the emancipation of slaves. He continued to convey this message until he died in 1895.

William and Ellen Craft, Disguised Fugitives

William and Ellen Craft were born into slavery. William's master, who was a gambler, sold off William's family in order to pay off his debts. Ellen was the daughter of an African American slave and her slave owner. Ellen had very light skin and was often mistaken for a member of her white family.

In 1846, William and Ellen were permitted to marry, but because they had different owners, they were not allowed to live together. They disliked being apart, so they began to save money and plan their escape to freedom.

In 1848, they escaped to Boston. Ellen used her light complexion to her advantage: she dressed up as a white man. Then she claimed that William was her slave. They traveled more than 1,000 miles by carriage, ship, and train to get to freedom in Boston and many thousands more to England to keep their freedom. They published their story in 1860 in a book titled *Running a Thousand Miles for Freedom*.

 Reading Passages

Leaders Before the Civil War *(cont.)*

Harriet Tubman, Underground Railroad Conductor

The greatest conductor of the Underground Railroad was a runaway slave known in history as Harriet Tubman. To the people she helped escape, she was known as Moses. Born one of eleven children in a slave family, she was mistreated and beaten by her master who often rented her out to other people. She was once hit on the head so hard by an overseer that she suffered from uncontrollable drowsiness or trances the rest of her life when she was not active. Hearing that she and two of her brothers were going to be sold to another owner, and probably sent to a state much deeper in the South, Harriet escaped alone. Her husband and brothers were unwilling to join her.

After stopping at several hideouts along the Underground Railroad in Maryland, Harriet arrived in Philadelphia in the free state of Pennsylvania. Determined to save her family, Harriet convinced leaders of the Underground Railroad to let her go back and rescue those she could, despite the great dangers she would face. In her first return trip to Maryland, Harriet spirited away her sister, Mary, and Mary's children, who were already on the auction block waiting to be sold.

Harriet tried to return and rescue her husband, but he had already remarried and refused to flee. Gradually, Harriet established a route of Underground Railroad stations and made over twenty trips into Southern states, rescuing two brothers, her parents, other members of her family, and more than 300 other slaves. Rewards for her capture posted by slave owners totaled over $40,000. Harriet carried a pistol on her secret missions and threatened to shoot anyone who refused to cooperate once they were on the run.

Harriet became a famous antislavery speaker and activist. She helped John Brown recruit some of his followers. During the Civil War, Harriet served as a spy, scout, and nurse for the Union army. She set up her own home as a refuge for needy freed slaves after the war.

☞ **$2,500** ☜
REWARD!

RANAWAY, from the Subscriber, residing in Dorchester County, Maryland State,
Negro Woman named HARRIET.

Leaders Before the Civil War *(cont.)*

Henry Bibb—He Never Quit

Henry Bibb was not a lucky man. He made his first effort to escape from slavery when he was twenty years old. He had seven different owners, most of them extremely brutal and cruel, and he tried to escape from each of them. He could have stayed free after several of his escapes, but he kept trying to return to Kentucky to help his wife, Malinda, and child, Mary Frances, escape to the North with him. He was always caught either by his owners or slave catchers and returned to captivity. Henry was routinely beaten and often saw his wife mistreated by owners who wanted to punish him by hurting his family. He was forced to wear irons and a bell by one owner.

During one escape attempt, he charged into a pack of hungry wolves with nothing but a knife to protect his family. One owner hated Henry so much that he refused to sell Henry's family to another slave buyer because Henry might somehow arrange their freedom. Despite many vicious beatings and severe punishments from a series of brutal owners, Henry did eventually escape to Canada and freedom, but he was never able to rescue his family. His wife finally told him that she no longer wanted to know him. However, he did help his mother and brothers get to Canada. Henry Bibb wrote the story of his life, *Narrative of the Life and Adventures of Henry Bibb, An American Slave,* before he died at the age of thirty-nine.

Other Leaders

There are many other stories of survival and hope in the face of huge obstacles. Harriet Ann Jacobs hid in a small, rat-infested attic for seven years in her successful effort to escape from her owner. Thousands of determined slaves followed the North Star and conductors of the Underground Railroad to reach freedom. Newspapermen Samuel Cornish and John Russwurm started the first African American newspaper, *Freedom's Journal.* James Forten became a wealthy businessman. Absolem Jones was a successful African American minister. Sojourner Truth spoke eloquently for the freedom of slaves and the rights of women.

Reading Passages

War, Reconstruction, and Segregation

Slavery Leads to War

Slavery in the Southern states was a crucial issue in the 1860 campaign for president of the United States. The Democratic Party split along regional lines with two candidates running. The new Republican Party nominated Abraham Lincoln, who was personally opposed to the institution of slavery but willing to tolerate it, if necessary, to keep the nation together. Lincoln was elected in a close race among four candidates. Before he even took office, Southern states fearing Lincoln's personal opposition to slavery began to secede from the Union. In 1861, Lincoln found himself leading the Northern states in a civil war that was created by the division over slavery. By 1862, he recognized that the entire issue of slavery had to be addressed.

African American Soldiers and Emancipation

By July 1862, Lincoln reluctantly accepted African Americans as soldiers in the Union army, although they were discriminated against in pay and other privileges and were led by white officers. More than 200,000 African Americans fought in the Union army and about 40,000 were killed. The Medal of Honor was awarded to twenty-three African American soldiers during the war. Lincoln also issued the Emancipation Proclamation on January 1, 1863, which freed slaves in areas under Confederate control when the Union army took control of an area in revolt. Although the proclamation freed no slaves immediately, it gradually led to the freedom of all slaves. African Americans called January 1, 1863, the Day of Jubilee.

Freedmen's Bureau and Reconstruction

In April 1865, Lee surrendered to Grant, and the war was essentially over. Lincoln was assassinated a few days later. In December 1865, the 13th Amendment to the U.S. Constitution officially ended slavery throughout the nation. The Reconstruction period of American history focused on helping the freed slaves and rebuilding from the war. The Freedmen's Bureau tried to help newly freed slaves adjust to independence. It issued food and essential supplies to freed African Americans; set up more than 100 hospitals; helped resettle more than 30,000 former slaves; and created 4,300 schools, several of which developed into prominent African American colleges, such as Fisk University and Howard University.

War, Reconstruction, and Segregation *(cont.)*

Black Codes and Reconstruction

Most African Americans were poor, unable to get jobs, and especially rejected and despised in the South. Southern state governments in 1865 and 1866 immediately set up black codes modeled on earlier slave codes that restricted African Americans from owning land and traveling. It even put jobless African Americans in jail. Despite the Civil Rights Act of 1866 and the 14th Amendment to the U.S. Constitution, which gave African Americans the full rights of citizenship, African Americans in the South were soon relegated to second-class status.

Violence and Poverty Subjugate African Americans

More than 5,000 African Americans were killed in the South in 1865 and 1866. Race riots, church and school burnings, and general violence orchestrated by the newly formed Ku Klux Klan gradually imposed brutal control over African Americans in the Southern states. Although some African Americans were elected to political office in the South during Reconstruction, they were never able to control the political process in any Southern state in order to help their people.

The alliance of African American political activists and Northern Republican carpetbaggers who moved south to promote their own political and economic interests provided some opportunity after the war.

Hiram Revels and Blanche Bruce were African American men elected to the U.S. Senate for a time. Lieutenant governors and other state officials were elected for brief periods in several Southern states.

The End of Reconstruction

By 1877, the loss of voting rights, which was due to local white control of the polls, led to the end of all political influence by African Americans and fierce control of all government, business, and public life by whites adamantly opposed to African American rights. The end of Reconstruction in 1877 saw African Americans totally dominated by white authority. Northern African Americans were freer, but they still faced discrimination in jobs, education, and living conditions.

Reading Passages

War, Reconstruction, and Segregation *(cont.)*

Jim Crow Laws

In the late 1800s, the Southern states relentlessly instituted legal restrictions, often called Jim Crow laws, on the rights of African Americans. They created poll taxes and literacy tests to prevent African Americans from voting in any elections. They required that railway passengers be separated by race. The U.S. Supreme Court issued a ruling in 1896 stating that segregation was not inherently unequal and that separate public facilities for the races were equal, although in practice African Americans always had the worst accommodations, parks, pools, schools, and other public facilities. By the early 1900s, all of the Southern states enforced racial segregation in schools, trains, churches, hotels, restaurants, theaters, and virtually all public places.

Violence and Lynching

The Ku Klux Klan and other violent gangs used beatings, threats, and murder to keep African Americans from trying to vote or resist the legal system of segregation. Thousands of African Americans were lynched (put to death illegally) by these gangs in the late 1800s and early 1900s. African Americans in the South were often forced into a form of legal bondage called *sharecropping*, where the families of former slaves were working on land owned by whites for which they received a share of the crop, if the crop was successful. These farmers usually ended up owing money to the white planters and living in a feudal situation not too different from slavery.

The Migration North in the 1900s

About one million African Americans migrated north in the decades from 1910 to 1930. Many found jobs in factories and in defense plants. Despite their best efforts to improve their economic situation, most of these migrants found they simply did not have the education and skills to find good jobs. Many ended up unemployed or doing very menial work for low pay as servants or day laborers. The new migrants were relegated to living in inner city slums called *ghettos*, which were plagued by crime, unsanitary living conditions, disease, and prejudice. Nonetheless, the North became a magnet for African Americans from the South desperate to better their lives. Many factory jobs were available, some children did attend integrated schools, many adults were able to vote, and living conditions offered more economic and political freedom than African Americans had experienced in the South. Life wasn't perfect, but it was better.

Reading Passages

War, Reconstruction, and Segregation *(cont.)*

World War I

More than 350,000 African Americans served in World War I where they encountered discrimination and mistreatment because of their race. Upon returning home from the war, these veterans wanted more equal treatment. This led to conflicts with whites who were often recruited by the Klan. More than twenty-five race riots occurred in the North in the aftermath of World War I.

New Leaders and Great Achievements

The period also saw the rise of prominent African Americans in literature, science, music, and political thought. The development of African American political groups, such as the National Association for the Advancement of Colored People (NAACP), the growth of African American colleges, the Harlem Renaissance of writers, and the birth of jazz can be attributed to many of these leaders.

The NAACP was formed by a group of African American leaders and some Northern white supporters to fight for racial equality using education, the law, public protests, and appeals to an American sense of fairness. African American leaders, such as Booker T. Washington and W. E. B. Du Bois, approached the needs of African Americans in different ways. Marcus Garvey moved his Universal Negro Improvement Association from Jamaica to Harlem in 1917 to foster pride among African Americans. He tried to establish a new African homeland for dispirited African Americans.

Musicians W. C. Handy, Louis Armstrong, and Duke Ellington created a distinct African American musical style characterized by the blues and jazz. Author Langston Hughes, poets Claude McKay and Countee Cullen, and many other writers helped create a literary rebirth in New York in the early 1900s—a time commonly known as the Harlem Renaissance. Olympic runner Jesse Owens and heavyweight boxer Joe Louis inspired many African American athletes. The Negro Leagues fostered baseball in the Northern cities in the 20th century.

The Depression

The Great Depression of the 1930s hit African Americans especially hard. They held less desirable jobs and were often the first to lose their jobs and homes. President Franklin Roosevelt reached out to African Americans and appointed educator Mary McLeod Bethune and a few other African American leaders to administrative jobs. Roosevelt's wife, Eleanor, became a passionate advocate for African American rights.

Reading
Passages

Leaders from the Civil War to the Great Depression

Ida B. Wells and Her Crusade for Justice

Ida B. Wells was born in 1862 to slave parents in Mississippi who were freed by the Union victory in the Civil War in 1865. Her father was a carpenter who could now be paid for his work by his former owner. He became a model for his young daughter when he refused to vote for the candidates his former owner supported and lost his job. Ida was the oldest in a large family and became the head of the family when her parents died of yellow fever. To support her brothers and sisters, Ida, at sixteen, became a country schoolteacher for poor, underfed African American children. The school was rundown and had few books and supplies. Later, she moved to Memphis, Tennessee, where she made more money teaching at a better school.

Ida joined a lyceum, a group of teachers who met to share poetry and ideas. She became the editor of the lyceum's journal and began to write. Ida began to be published in other newspapers because her essays spoke out against the injustices endured by African Americans. Storeowners and political leaders were creating a system of deep segregation. Stores, restaurants, hotels, and train cars could deny access to African Americans. Newly passed Jim Crow laws made these actions legal. Ida was forced off a railroad car because of her race and sued the company. She won the case in a lower court but later was defeated by the railroad company in the Tennessee Supreme Court.

Journalist and Advocate

Ida wrote for an African American journal called the *Memphis Free Speech*, in which she campaigned against Jim Crow laws and gave practical advice to her readers. While Ida was away on a business trip, her close friend was arrested for trying to defend his store against a gang of whites. He was arrested and jailed instead of the white gang. While in jail, another mob of white men took him and other African Americans out of jail and lynched them. This incident spurred Ida's long newspaper campaign against lynching. The newspaper offices of the *Memphis Free Speech* were destroyed after Ida encouraged African Americans to leave the state and head west to avoid the violence and mistreatment they encountered.

Reading Passages

Leaders from the Civil War to the Great Depression *(cont.)*

Ida B. Wells and Her Crusade for Justice *(cont.)*

Ida moved to New York and wrote for an influential African American newspaper called the *New York Age*. Her articles crusaded against lynching and ended with her signature line, "Yours for justice, Ida B. Wells." She became the editor of a Chicago newspaper owned by her husband whom she married in 1895. She continued her campaign against lynching and other injustices until her death in 1931. In the 1880s, as many as 185 African Americans were murdered by lynch mobs in one year. A few years before her death, the number had dropped to twenty-five per year.

W. E. B. Du Bois, Founder, NAACP

"The human soul cannot be permanently chained." These words were a guiding light expressed by William Edward Burghardt Du Bois, born in Massachusetts in 1868, three years after the end of the American Civil War. He was one of the most important intellectual leaders of the African American community for seventy years. He attended Fisk University, a school for African Americans in the intensely segregated state of Tennessee. He never forgot the instances of prejudice he encountered in the South—the separate and inferior facilities for African Americans, the lynchings and legal mistreatment of his people, and the efforts to keep them in ignorance and poverty. Du Bois finished his academic education at Harvard University in Boston. In 1895, he became the first African American to receive a Ph.D. in the United States.

Teacher, Author, and African American Spokesman

Du Bois taught at two African American colleges—Wilberforce in Ohio and Atlanta in Georgia—and wrote sixteen books about his research demonstrating the equality of the races if the opportunities for education were equal. His publication of *The Souls of Black Folk*—a book of essays protesting segregation, racism, and Jim Crow laws—made him a leader in the movement for equality. He opposed the less aggressive and conciliatory tactics of Booker T. Washington, then the leading spokesman for African Americans in the country.

Reading Passages

Leaders from the Civil War to the Great Depression *(cont.)*

W. E. B. Du Bois, Founder, NAACP *(cont.)*

Du Bois founded a group called the Niagara Movement that eventually created the National Association for the Advancement of Colored People (NAACP) in 1910. He edited *The Crisis*, the NAACP magazine, for twenty-five years. He used the magazine to expose instances of prejudice and mistreatment of African Americans in all walks of life. The NAACP became a major organization in the fight for equality in the United States.

In his later years, Du Bois became involved in the Pan-African movement to liberate the former African colonies from European control. At the end of his life, Du Bois became a citizen of Ghana and was buried not far from the dock where slaves had been sent to America centuries before.

Booker T. Washington, Founder, Tuskegee Institute

Booker T. Washington was born a slave in Virginia and was freed with the end of the Civil War. As a boy, he worked as a coal miner and in a salt mine. Booker had always wanted to attend school and finally got the opportunity when a school opened in his community. He had no legal last name to tell the teacher, so he decided to call himself Booker Washington. In his teen years, Booker worked on the household staff of a general's wife, who gave him books and lessons in hard work, cleanliness, and frugality in spending money—lessons that he later taught at Tuskegee.

To attend Hampton Institute, an industrial school for African Americans, Booker walked, jumped railroad cars, and hitched buggy rides for 300 miles. He arrived dirty and disheveled and made a poor impression on the teachers, but he was able to work his way through school as a janitor. This trade school taught reading, writing, and arithmetic, and also carpentry, tailoring, and farming. They stressed proper behavior, thrift, and self-discipline. Washington came to believe, as Hampton Institute's leaders did, that the African American working class would provide leadership for African Americans and allow them to succeed in a white-dominated society, just as it had worked for immigrants new to America.

Reading Passages

Leaders from the Civil War to the Great Depression *(cont.)*

Booker T. Washington, Founder, Tuskegee Institute *(cont.)*

When he finished school, Booker taught at Hampton Institute for a few years before he founded Tuskegee Normal and Industrial School as a place for African Americans to learn trades, such as carpentry, farming, and teaching. Washington started his school with a few broken down farm buildings and land he bought for $500. He, the faculty, and the students built much of the school themselves. Booker hired George Washington Carver to teach better farming techniques at Tuskegee. Carver's many new uses for crops and his farming innovations added to the school's growing reputation. Washington married three times (his first two wives died young), and all of his wives were major forces as teachers at Tuskegee.

Advisor to Presidents

Washington was convinced that African Americans could only succeed if they had desirable skills that would get them good jobs. He felt they needed to be economically successful before they could achieve equality with whites and overcome the effects of poverty, legal segregation, and discrimination. Washington was popular with many Southern whites because he did not advocate immediate equality. He advised two presidents, Theodore Roosevelt and William Howard Taft, about African American concerns and political appointments.

The Atlanta Compromise

Booker T. Washington carried on a heated battle with W. E. B. Du Bois over the issue of challenging segregation and becoming active opponents of white domination of African Americans, especially in the South. Washington often told whites they needed to hire African Americans and pay them fairly. He told both groups that African Americans and whites should work together.

Many African Americans opposed his "Atlanta Compromise," which he proposed at an Atlanta exposition designed to promote agriculture and trade in the South. Washington said, "In all things that are purely social we can be as separate as the fingers, yet one as the hand in all things essential to mutual progress." His opponents believed that compromise with the rigid segregation of the South would result in further harm to their people and no end to second-class citizenship.

Reading Passages

African American Heroes, 1865–1940

Matthew Henson, Arctic Explorer

"I think I'm the first man to sit on top of the world," Matthew Henson told Robert Peary, his longtime companion and the leader of a series of expeditions to reach the exact geographic location of the North Pole. Their explorations together had spanned nearly twenty years. Peary was a United States naval officer who was able to get financial support from wealthy and important people anxious to be involved in the first expedition to the North Pole.

In 1887, Matthew Henson, who had sailed as a cabin boy to many lands in Europe, Africa, and Asia, was hired as a personal servant to Robert Peary, who was then trying to map a canal route through Nicaragua. Henson impressed Peary with his hard work and seafaring skills. In 1891, Peary hired Henson again to accompany him on an expedition to Greenland. His goal was to map the unknown areas of that island and to reach the North Pole.

Together, they would spend eighteen years on eight expeditions before they reached their goal.

Commander Peary raised the money and possessed the influence and navigational skills needed for the mission. Matthew Henson was just as essential to the ultimate success of the mission. He quickly learned from their Inuit (American Indian) companions how to survive and travel in the freezing Arctic weather. He became an expert dog-sled driver in blinding blizzards, over moving ice packs, and around dangerous rivers of freezing ice and water. He learned to hunt the native musk oxen and other animals needed to feed the members of the expedition. He learned to speak the native languages of the Inuit and became a respected friend and colleague of these proud Arctic residents.

On April 6, 1909, after several expeditions combining dangerous sea travel and long sled trips through bitter Arctic storms, Peary, Henson, and four Inuit men reached the top of the world.

Reading
Passages

African American Heroes, 1865–1940 (cont.)

Recognition at Last

There were several years of controversy with the conflicting claims of another explorer before geographers and scientists were convinced of the group's achievement. Peary received numerous awards from the United States government and private scientific societies. Henson (and their four Inuit companions) was largely ignored until the 1940s when Henson's achievements and the extraordinary value of his work was recognized. In 1988, thirty-three years after his death, Matthew Henson was reburied next to Robert Peary in Arlington National Cemetery.

Bill Pickett, Rodeo Cowboy

Cowboys are usually portrayed as white in books and movies, but at least one-third of the cowboys in Texas were African American. African American cowboys were also common in other western states. One of the most famous of these men was Bill Pickett, a son of former slaves who was fascinated as a child by the cowboy life. Pickett worked for local ranchers in Texas as a young boy and became an expert horseman, skilled in training wild horses from the Texas plains. Pickett soon became known for a new way of controlling wild cattle. He would grab a wild steer by the horns and wrestle it to the ground. Often, he would bite the steer's lip to control the animal. This soon developed into a rodeo contest called *bulldogging*.

With his brothers, Bill Pickett started his own business called Pickett Brothers Bronco Busters and Rough Riders. They worked for local ranchers.

Bill later joined local rodeos, and in 1907, he performed in a famous wild west show where he rode horses and wrestled steers. He worked in many shows in the United States and even performed in England before the king and queen. Bill later worked with his friend, Will Rogers, a famous rodeo and radio entertainer of the time. In 1921, Bill Pickett became the first African American cowboy to perform in his own movie called *The Bull-Dogger*. He acted in several other movies, as well.

Bill was hurt in several rodeo accidents, especially one in Mexico City. World War I also interrupted his rodeo and acting career. He died in April 1932 after getting kicked in the head by a horse. In 1971, he became the first African American cowboy accepted in the National Rodeo Cowboy Hall of Fame.

Reading Passages

African American Heroes, 1865–1940 *(cont.)*

Charles Drew, Blood Expert

Charles Richard Drew was born on June 3, 1904, in an area of Washington, D.C., called Foggy Bottom. His father was a carpet layer, and his mother was a schoolteacher who had attended Howard University, an African American college in Washington, D.C. His grandparents' heritage included African, American Indian, and British roots. In his youth, Charles sold newspapers, worked on construction projects, and did factory work. In church, he was strongly influenced to serve his community. Drew attended the only high school that offered college preparatory classes for African American students.

Charles was accepted at Amherst College on a partial scholarship. He was a strong athlete and was an excellent student. While he was hospitalized for a severe football injury, he observed a blood transfusion and became very interested in medicine. Charles graduated with honors from Amherst in 1926, taught at Morgan State College in Maryland for two years, and saved enough money to enter medical school at McGill University in Montreal, Canada. In 1933, he graduated at the top of his class as a doctor of medicine and a master of surgery.

Drew became very interested in the problems involved in blood transfusions, a process for providing blood to critically ill or wounded patients. In transfusions, patients must have the same type of blood.

Drew worked for two more years in the hospital at McGill University. Drew went home to Washington, D.C., after his father's death and worked for three years at Howard University as a teacher and as a doctor at Freedmen's Hospital, a hospital founded for freed African Americans after the Civil War. In 1938, Drew received a fellowship to do advanced research in blood chemistry and transfusions at Columbia University. He became director of the hospital blood bank in 1939. In 1940, Drew became the first African American to earn a doctor of science in medicine degree. His specialty was blood preservation and blood banking.

Reading Passages

African American Heroes, 1865–1940 *(cont.)*

Charles Drew, Blood Expert *(cont.)*

Whole blood contains four elements. Red blood cells determine the different types of blood (A, B, AB, and O), but they are the part of blood that breaks down within twenty-four hours. The other three elements are white blood cells, platelets, and plasma. Drew decided to experiment with plasma, which can be given to any person regardless of blood type. It can be stored for a month, dried, and even frozen for a year. Drew made it possible to store blood safely, which became essential to the nation and the world because World War II created a need for countless blood transfusions due to the massive war casualties. Charles Drew developed the first blood banks in New York City by using hospitals and refrigerated trucks for mobile blood banks. He soon helped the Red Cross open blood banks all over the country.

Drew tried to resist the decision of the Red Cross to segregate the blood of African Americans and whites, despite the fact that no differences exist between races in blood composition. He argued against the bigotry of the American Medical Association, which would not accept African American doctors who were therefore prevented from working in white hospitals.

On April 1, 1950, Dr. Drew died in an automobile accident in North Carolina, while on his way to a medical conference in Tuskegee, Alabama. He was given transfusions, but he was too badly injured to survive. The discoveries made by Charles Drew and the doctors he taught will extend his influence for generations.

Many Heroes and Heroines

There were many more African American heroes and heroines of the period. Singer Marian Anderson combated prejudice with her voice and character. Biologist George Washington Carver (see page 67) invented many products and reformed Southern farming techniques. Sarah B. Walker became a successful business woman who provided jobs for many women and donated large amounts of money for campaigns against lynching and for other African American needs. There were many more heroes and heroines of this predominantly painful period of history.

Reading Passages

The Civil Rights Movement, 1945–1970

The Beginning of the Movement

The events in the early 20th century set the stage for the civil rights movement of the 1950s and 1960s. More than 1,000,000 African Americans served during World War II, usually in segregated units. The experiences of discrimination in the service and combat led many of the African American veterans to want greater equality and opportunity when the war ended.

Between 1940 and 1970 in another African American migration from the South, more than four million African American Southerners moved north hoping for better opportunity. They joined more than one million African Americans who had migrated north from 1910 to 1930. Northern cities developed huge ghettos where African Americans found they were still segregated and subjected to second-class citizenship, although there was greater personal freedom, fewer humiliations, and more opportunities for better jobs and lives than in the South.

Brown v. Board of Education

The first victory in the civil rights movement came with the unanimous ruling by the Supreme Court against segregation in public schools in 1954. Several challenges to segregated schools were combined in this case, and the court's ruling that separate is not equal undermined the legal basis of segregation in public education. Unfortunately, it did not set a deadline for correcting the injustice.

This ruling created a huge white backlash against African Americans in much of the South. A hate group called the White Citizens' Council (WCC) had chapters in many Southern cities with the intent of punishing African Americans economically if they tried to advocate desegregation in any manner.

Emmett Till's Murder

In August 1955, Emmett Till, a fourteen-year-old African American boy visiting relatives in Mississippi, was viciously murdered for allegedly whistling at a white woman in a store. The boy's open-casket funeral drew 50,000 mourners and became a symbol of the mistreatment of African Americans. His killers were set free by an all-white jury.

Reading Passages

The Civil Rights Movement, 1945–1970 *(cont.)*

The Montgomery Bus Boycott

In December of 1955, Rosa Parks refused to give up her seat on a Montgomery public bus to a white man. Her refusal sparked a boycott led by the Reverend Ralph Abernathy and Dr. Martin Luther King Jr. For a year, African Americans refused to ride the buses in the city. Instead, they walked to work, rode with friends and employers in some cases, and became the true spark for the civil rights movement. The protesters practiced Dr. King's policy of meeting violence with non-violence. In December of 1956, the Supreme Court ruled that segregation on city buses was unconstitutional. The Montgomery bus system almost went bankrupt because of the loss of riders. The leaders of the movement founded the Southern Christian Leadership Conference (SCLC) to carry on the work of national desegregation.

Sit-ins

In September 1957, nine brave African American teenagers faced mobs, armed police, and National Guard troops in order to attend all-white Central High School in Little Rock, Arkansas. In February 1960, four African American college students held a sit-in at a segregated lunch counter in Greensboro, North Carolina. Their actions led to sit-ins at lunch counters and other public places, such as libraries, museums, and parks in other states. Gradually, these activities succeeded in ending segregation at these establishments.

Freedom Riders and Other Protests

Freedom riders, both African American and white, rode through the South on buses to enforce a legal decision that segregation on interstate transportation was illegal. The riders were attacked by white mobs in Alabama, jailed, and beaten. In September 1961, the U.S. Attorney General outlawed segregation on interstate buses.

Dr. King was arrested in Birmingham, along with hundreds of demonstrators protesting segregation in Birmingham department stores. As many as 1,000 demonstrations were held throughout the South in 1963, and over 20,000 civil rights workers were jailed.

Reading Passages

The Civil Rights Movement, 1945–1970 *(cont.)*

The March on Washington

To help Americans appreciate the importance of civil rights for all, a march on Washington was held on August 28, 1963. Dr. Martin Luther King Jr. delivered his famous "I Have a Dream" speech, which resonated with many Americans the need for equal rights for African Americans. Violence continued against African Americans in September of 1963, when four young girls were killed in a church bombing in Birmingham, Alabama.

Civil Rights Act of 1964

In July 1964, President Johnson signed the Civil Rights Act of 1964, which insured fair employment and the right to use public facilities and protected the voting rights of African Americans. However, many Southern states refused to obey the law, and Dr. King and other leaders protested the actions of these unwilling states. Freedom Summer, a voter registration campaign, led to violence by gangs of whites and police

against demonstrators. The walk from Selma to Montgomery, Alabama, led by Dr. King, began as a memorial march for one of the victims of the violence.

Selma Violence

People throughout the nation watched on television in horror and outrage when 600 peaceful protesters were attacked on a bridge in Selma by troopers and mounted police using nightsticks, tear gas, whips, and other weapons. National outrage over these brutal tactics, as well as the use of dogs and fire hoses against protesters, led to the passage of the landmark Voting Rights Act of 1965, which provided tough federal protection of voting rights for African Americans.

A Broader Movement

Dr. King and other civil rights leaders broadened their aims and targeted discrimination in the North as well as the South. The assassination of Dr. Martin Luther King Jr. in 1968 led to riots in many cities in the summer of 1968. The movement for equal rights for African Americans continued and split into several factions. Today, people of all races and ethnic minorities benefit from the pioneer work of the civil rights movement, and African Americans have successfully entered mainstream politics at every level, from the grassroots of local political jobs to the United States presidency.

Reading Passages

Moments and Movers in the Civil Rights Movement

Thurgood Marshall, Man of Law

Thurgood Marshall graduated from Howard University School of Law and soon became a lawyer working for the National Association for the Advancement of Colored People (NAACP). In 1935, he won a decision allowing an African American to enter the University of Maryland School of Law. In 1940, he argued his first decision before the United States Supreme Court. He would eventually win twenty-nine of thirty-two cases he argued before the highest court in the land. His greatest legal achievement was his successful challenge to segregation in public schools when he won the landmark case, *Brown v. Board of Education*, in 1954. This unanimous decision was the first crack in the system of segregation imposed in many Southern states. In 1967, President Lyndon B. Johnson appointed Thurgood Marshall as the first African American justice on the Supreme Court.

Rosa Parks and The Montgomery Bus Boycott

Rosa Parks was tired—in body, mind, and spirit—as she left her work as a seamstress on December 1, 1955, and boarded a bus in Montgomery, Alabama. Rosa gave her money to the driver, got off the bus, as African Americans were required to do, and then reentered at the back of the bus. She hoped the rear section reserved for African American customers would have a free seat. It was always crowded, while the white section was often empty or had few patrons.

On entering the bus, it was obvious that all the "colored" seats were occupied, but there was a free seat in the "neutral" section, a middle part of the bus that anyone could use. She was seated and resting when the bus driver screamed at her to leave her seat for a white man who wanted to sit there. The other African Americans in the neutral seats had already moved.

Rosa was tired of deferring to whites—tired of segregated restrooms, separate drinking fountains, different parks, second-rate schools, and segregated buses. She refused to move, despite the driver's threats. He called the police, and she was arrested, tried, convicted of her "crime." She was fined $10 plus $4 in court costs. At the time, Rosa only earned $23 a week as a seamstress.

Reading Passages

Moments and Movers in the Civil Rights Movement *(cont.)*

Dr. King Leads the Boycott

Parks' actions served as the flash point of a determined drive by the African American citizens of Montgomery to force a change in policy. They organized in their churches and communities and decided to boycott the buses in the city until the law was changed. They got the brilliant and charismatic preacher, Dr. Martin Luther King Jr., to lead the boycott. African American citizens altered their transportation routines. Most walked—from Dec. 2, 1955 until November 13, 1956—while Parks' conviction was appealed through the court system. On November 13, 1956, the Supreme Court of the United States ruled in Parks' favor. It said the Constitution of the United States makes no provision for second-class status and that all Americans are equal under the law. Rosa Parks continued her involvement in civil rights for the rest of her life.

Martin Luther King Jr., Civil Rights Champion

Martin Luther King Jr. was born into a family active in Baptist church ministry. Dr. King entered Morehouse College at the age of fifteen and was ordained at the age of nineteen. He received a B.A. in Divinity at Crozer Theological Seminary.

During his years at Crozer, Dr. King studied the philosophy of nonviolent protest used by Mohandas Gandhi.

Dr. King was the pastor of the Dexter Avenue Baptist Church in Atlanta when he was asked to organize and lead the Montgomery bus boycott in 1955. His extraordinary eloquence and ability to mobilize the community thrust him into the forefront of the civil rights movement. He became a national symbol of African American hopes—both hated by his enemies and admired by those who supported his goals.

Ralph Abernathy, Freedom's Preacher

The Reverend Ralph Abernathy was a major figure in the civil rights movement, and he was, in a sense, present to help light the fuse of the movement. Ralph Abernathy and Dr. Martin Luther King Jr. were the men who organized the Montgomery bus boycott and kept it going for a year. After the successful bus boycott, Dr. Abernathy led marches aimed at ending discrimination and securing voting rights for African Americans in Selma and Birmingham, Alabama; Albany, Georgia; and Washington, D.C. He was with Dr. King when King was shot, and he continued his work after King's murder. "You can kill the dreamer," he said, "but you cannot kill the dream."

The Little Rock Nine

On September 4, 1957, six African American girls and three boys tried to legally attend Central High School in Little Rock, Arkansas. They were met by an angry white mob and the Arkansas National Guard armed with guns. The nine African American students were turned away while the nation watched on television. Three weeks later, they entered the school protected by federal troops ordered there by President Eisenhower. In the next few years, the nine graduated from Central High. Their names were Minnijean Brown, Elizabeth Eckford, Thelma Mothershed, Gloria Ray, Carlotta Walls, Melba Pattillo, Terrence Roberts, Jefferson Thomas, and Ernest Green.

Reading Passages

Moments and Movers in the Civil Rights Movement *(cont.)*

The Greensboro Four

On February 1, 1960, four freshmen students at an all-African American college in Greensboro, North Carolina, staged a sit-in at a segregated lunch counter in a Woolworth store in the same city. They were refused service, and they peacefully refused to leave. News of this quiet and peaceful protest soon spread throughout many states, and sit-ins were staged at segregated lunch counters in many cities.

The peaceful protesters were attacked, spit upon, cursed, insulted, and some were even burned with cigarettes. Food and soda were spilled on them, and they were forcibly removed. Other protesters took their places. Some lunch counters were soon integrated, and the movement to desegregate all counters spread. The four men in the very first sit-in were Ezell Blair Jr., Franklin McCain, Joseph McNeil, and David Richmond. By the summer of 1962, the first lunch counter where they began their protest was integrated.

Medgar Evers Wanted to Vote

Medgar Evers had far-reaching memories of discrimination and brutality toward African Americans in his native Mississippi. After serving in France and Germany during World War II, he returned to Mississippi determined to vote on Election Day. He and his friends ignored threats by whites to stay out of town and were met by a mob of armed men who stopped them from voting. Evers became a leader in the Mississippi chapter of the NAACP and led meetings, marches, boycotts, and other demonstrations for civil rights and equal education for African Americans in Mississippi. He was beaten by white gangs, and his home was firebombed. On June 12, 1963, he was murdered by a gunman after a church meeting. His example and influence, however, led other African Americans in Mississippi to continue the struggle.

Fannie Lou Hamer and the Right to Vote

Fannie Lou Hamer was born the youngest of twenty children in a sharecropper family in rural Mississippi. Her family all worked on white-owned plantations picking cotton and doing farm work from daybreak to dark just to get enough to eat. When she grew up and married a sharecropper, Fannie became determined to do something to break the system of degradation, humiliation, and poverty that plagued all African Americans, especially those in Mississippi.

Reading Passages

Moments and Movers in the Civil Rights Movement *(cont.)*

Fannie Lou Hamer and the Right to Vote *(cont.)*

In 1962, members of the Student Nonviolent Coordinating Committee visited Mississippi to encourage African Americans to register to vote. Fannie became convinced that voting was the key needed to open the door to equal rights. She was turned down three times when the white registrar of elections claimed she failed a literacy test. When Fannie did finally pass the test, they refused to let her vote because she had no money to pay a poll tax, another obstacle used by the white authorities to prevent African Americans from voting.

Fannie was ordered off the plantation where she and her husband were sharecropping. She hid in a neighbor's home that was shot at by angry whites. Fannie became involved in organizing African Americans in rural Mississippi. She held meetings, preached in churches, and led voter registration marches. She and members of her group were arrested and brutally beaten in jail. Fannie helped create the Mississippi Freedom Democratic Party (MFDP) to help African Americans be represented in Mississippi politics because the regular Democratic party would not admit African Americans.

Fannie managed to register 63,000 African Americans in the MFDP. She and the new party gained national attention in 1964 when they tried to be represented in the National Democratic Presidential Convention. Fannie gave a dramatic speech at the convention describing the dreams and hopes of African Americans and the many obstacles her people had overcome to be represented.

She and the new party lost at that convention, but when they returned to the party convention in 1968 with even greater support in Mississippi, they were finally seated.

Many Leaders

Many other leaders helped propel the civil rights movement. John Lewis led freedom rides throughout the South and was at the front of the march in Selma. He became a U.S. Congressman, representing Georgia, in 1987. James Meredith successfully appealed to the Supreme Court to force the University of Mississippi Law School to accept him. The Reverend Fred Shuttlesworth led a movement to desegregate buses and schools in Birmingham, Alabama, despite having his home firebombed and his wife struck with a knife. Six-year-old Ruby Bridges was escorted to a New Orleans school by federal marshals. The list of civil rights heroes, many little known, is long and includes people of many faiths and backgrounds.

African Americans in Early America Quiz

Directions: Read pages 7–11 about African American life and personalities in early America. Answer these questions based on the information in the selection. Circle the correct answer to each question below. Underline the sentence in the selection where the answer is found.

1. Where did most slaves in the American colonies come from?

   a. South Africa
   b. Europe
   c. West Africa
   d. East Africa

2. About how many free African Americans lived in the United States in 1860?

   a. one million
   b. four million
   c. half a million
   d. two million

3. Who walked across Texas and down the Pacific coast of Mexico?

   a. Jean DuSable
   b. Esteban the Black
   c. Phillis Wheatley
   d. Benjamin Banneker

4. Which of these products was used to purchase slaves in Africa?

   a. guns
   b. rum
   c. tobacco
   d. all of the above

5. What was the "Middle Passage"?
   a. slave ship voyage to America
   b. voyage to Europe
   c. tribal warfare
   d. slave ship name

6. Which law made it necessary for slaves to reach Canada before they were safe from recapture?
   a. Missouri Compromise
   b. Fugitive Slave Law
   c. *Dred Scott* Decision
   d. Middle Passage

7. Who founded Chicago and ran a trading post there?
   a. Phillis Wheatley
   b. Jean DuSable
   c. Benjamin Banneker
   d. Esteban the Black

8. Which American leader was a vocal opponent of slavery?
   a. George Washington
   b. Thomas Jefferson
   c. Susannah Wheatley
   d. John Quincy Adams

9. Who helped design the city of Washington, D.C.?
   a. Benjamin Franklin
   b. Benjamin Banneker
   c. Phillis Wheatley
   d. both a and b

10. About how many slaves lived in the South in 1860?
    a. forty million

    b. half a million
    c. twenty-three million
    d. four million

Leaders Before the Civil War Quiz

Directions: Read pages 12–16 about African American leaders before the Civil War. Answer these questions based on the information in the selection. Circle the correct answer to each question below. Underline the sentence in the selection where the answer is found.

1. Which of these men was a mountain man?
   a. Nat Turner
   b. Frederick Douglass
   c. Henry Bibb
   d. James Beckwourth

2. Who asked James Beckwourth to help negotiate a peace treaty with the Crow Indians?
   a. Cheyenne Indians
   b. General Ashley
   c. the U.S. Army
   d. Blackfoot Indians

3. Who taught Nat Turner to read?
   a. his mother
   b. no one
   c. Benjamin Turner
   d. both a and c

4. Who became convinced that he was chosen by God to lead a rebellion against slave owners?
   a. Nat Turner
   b. Frederick Douglass
   c. Henry Bibb
   d. William Craft

5. Which conductor of the Underground Railroad was also a spy, scout, and nurse for the Union army in the Civil War?
   a. Henry Bibb
   b. Frederick Douglass
   c. Harriet Tubman
   d. Nat Turner

6. Who discovered a pass through the Sierra Nevada Mountains to the Long Valley in California?
   a. William and Ellen Craft
   b. Frederick Douglass
   c. James Beckwourth
   d. Harriet Tubman

7. Who led more than 300 slaves to freedom along hideouts on the Underground Railroad?
   a. Harriet Tubman
   b. William and Ellen Craft
   c. Henry Bibb
   d. Frederick Douglass

8. Who traveled over 1,000 miles to freedom with her husband who pretended to be her slave?
   a. Harriet Tubman
   b. Ellen Craft
   c. Malinda Bibb
   d. Harriet Jacobs

9. About how many armed slave owners and state militia were trying to stop Nat Turner?
   a. 18
   b. 60
   c. 3,000
   d. 1,831

10. Which of these people wrote a book?
   a. Nat Turner
   b. Harriet Tubman
   c. Henry Bibb
   d. all of the above

War, Reconstruction, and Segregation Quiz

Directions: Read pages 17–20 about African American life between the Civil War and World War I. Answer these questions based on the information in the selection. Circle the correct answer to each question below. Underline the sentence in the selection where the answer is found.

1. Which organization tried to help newly freed slaves adjust to independence?

   a. black codes

   b. Freedmen's Bureau

   c. Ku Klux Klan

   d. all of the above

2. Which of these people was part of the Harlem Renaissance, a group of popular and skilled writers?

   a. Langston Hughes

   b. Marcus Garvey

   c. Louis Armstrong

   d. Jesse Owens

3. About how many African Americans migrated North between 1910 and 1930?

   a. 350,000

   b. one million

   c. 200,000

   d. 30,000

4. When was the Day of Jubilee for African Americans?

   a. January 1, 1865

   b. January 1, 1863

   c. April 1, 1865

   d. December 31, 1877

5. What year did Reconstruction end?

   a. 1877

   b. 1866

   c. 1896

   d. 1930

6. Why did African Americans migrate North between 1910 and 1930?

   a. better jobs

   b. integrated schools

   c. more freedom

   d. all of the above

7. Which president's wife became an advocate for African Americans?

   a. Theodore Roosevelt

   b. Franklin Roosevelt

   c. Herbert Hoover

   d. Jim Crow

8. What name was given to Northern politicians who went South to promote their own political and financial interests?

   a. Klansmen

   b. sharecroppers

   c. freedmen

   d. carpetbaggers

9. Which laws created poll taxes and literacy tests to keep African Americans in the South from voting?

   a. Jim Crow laws

   b. black codes

   c. 13th amendment

   d. Freedmen's Bureau

10. What group used lynching and other forms of violence to enforce segregation?

   a. sharecroppers

   b. carpetbaggers

   c. Ku Klux Klan

   d. NAACP

Leaders from the Civil War to the Great Depression Quiz

Directions: Read pages 21–24 about African American leaders between the Civil War and the Great Depression. Answer these questions based on the information in the selection. Circle the correct answer to each question below. Underline the sentence in the selection where the answer is found.

1. Which leader proposed the "Atlanta Compromise"?
   a. Booker T. Washington
   b. Ida B. Wells
   c. W. E. B. Du Bois
   d. George Washington Carver

2. Who wrote many newspaper articles against lynching?
   a. Ida B. Wells
   b. Booker T. Washington
   c. W. E. B. Du Bois
   d. both a and b

3. Who was an advisor to Presidents Roosevelt and Taft?
   a. Booker T. Washington
   b. Ida B. Wells
   c. W. E. B. Du Bois
   d. George Washington Carver

4. What is the name for a group of people who share poetry and ideas?
   a. court
   b. essay
   c. lyceum
   d. journal

5. What were the *Memphis Free Speech* and the *New York Age*?
   a. radio news reports
   b. teen magazines
   c. newspapers
   d. books

6. Who was a founder of the NAACP?
   a. W. E. B. Du Bois
   b. Booker T. Washington
   c. Tuskegee Institute
   d. William Howard Taft

7. Which of these publications was a magazine published by the NAACP?
   a. *Memphis Free Speech*
   b. *New York Age*
   c. *New York Times*
   d. *The Crisis*

8. Who was buried in Africa near a dock where slaves were shipped to America?
   a. Ida B. Wells
   b. Booker T. Washington
   c. Jim Crow
   d. W. E. B. Du Bois

9. Who openly opposed Jim Crow laws and all forms of segregation?
   a. Ida B. Wells
   b. Booker T. Washington
   c. W. E. B. Du Bois
   d. both a and c

10. Who was forced to leave a segregated rail car and sued the company?
    a. Ida B. Wells
    b. Booker T. Washington
    c. George W. Carver
    d. W. E. B. Du Bois

African American Heroes, 1865–1940 Quiz

Directions: Read pages 25–28 about African American heroes between 1865 and 1940. Answer these questions based on the information in the selection. Circle the correct answer to each question below. Underline the sentence in the selection where the answer is found.

1. How many years did Commander Peary and Matthew Henson work together to reach the North Pole?

    a. nine

    b. twenty-two

    c. eighteen

    d. two

2. What is the word used to describe biting a steer on the lip while wrestling it to the ground?

    a. Inuit

    b. rodeo

    c. surgery

    d. bulldogging

3. Who is buried in Arlington National Cemetery?

    a. Charles Drew

    b. Robert Peary

    c. Matthew Henson

    d. both b and c

4. Which of these are the four main blood types?

    a. types A, B, C, D

    b. types A, B, C, O

    c. types O, A, B, AB

    d. types E, O, AB, B

5. What did the Red Cross insist on doing with blood during World War II?

    a. refuse African American donors

    b. segregate blood by race

    c. refuse to store blood

    d. all of the above

6. Who accompanied Commander Peary when he reached the North Pole?

    a. Matthew Henson

    b. four Inuit men

    c. Charles Drew

    d. both a and b

7. Which college did Dr. Charles Drew attend?

    a. McGill University

    b. Amherst College

    c. Columbia University

    d. all of the above

8. Who was the first African American to earn a doctor of science in medicine degree?

    a. Robert Peary

    b. Charles Drew

    c. George W. Carver

    d. Bill Pickett

9. Who was a bronco buster and rough rider?

    a. Bill Pickett

    b. Charles Drew

    c. Matthew Henson

    d. all of the above

10. What dangers did Matthew Henson have to overcome on his Arctic trips?

    a. snakes

    b. freezing rivers

    c. moving ice packs

    d. both b and c

1500   1550   1600   1650   1700   1750   1800   1850   1900   1950   2000

The Civil Rights Movement, 1945–1970 Quiz

Directions: Read pages 29–31 about the civil rights movement from 1945 to 1970. Answer these questions based on the information in the selection. Circle the correct answer to each question below. Underline the sentence in the selection where the answer is found.

1. Which president signed the Civil Rights Act of 1964?
   a. John F. Kennedy
   b. Lyndon B. Johnson
   c. Richard Nixon
   d. Bill Clinton

2. Why did Emmett Till get murdered?
   a. He allegedly robbed a store.
   b. He allegedly whistled at a white woman.
   c. He allegedly was a freedom rider.
   d. He allegedly attacked a police officer.

3. Where were sit-ins held?
   a. lunch counters
   b. libraries
   c. museums
   d. all of the above

4. In what state were freedom riders attacked, jailed, and beaten?
   a. New York
   b. Alabama
   c. North Carolina
   d. Arkansas

5. Where were four young girls killed in a church bombing?
   a. Selma
   b. Montgomery
   c. Birmingham
   d. Atlanta

6. How many Southern African Americans moved North between 1940 and 1970?
   a. one million
   b. 50,000
   c. 600
   d. more than four million

7. Why did people throughout most of America get angry at the police behavior in Selma?
   a. They read about it.
   b. They heard about it from friends.
   c. They saw it on television.
   d. They heard about it from their employers.

8. About how many civil rights workers were jailed in the demonstrations held in the South in 1963?
   a. 1,000
   b. 2,000
   c. 20,000
   d. 600

9. Where was Dr. King's "I Have a Dream" speech delivered?
   a. Birmingham
   b. Montgomery
   c. Selma
   d. Washington, D.C.

10. How did African Americans protest discrimination?
   a. sit-ins
   b. freedom rides
   c. marches
   d. all of the above

©*Teacher Created Resources*   41   *#3395 African Americans*

Moments and Movers in the Civil Rights Movement Quiz

Directions: Read pages 32–35 about special people and events in the civil rights movement. Answer these questions based on the information in the selection. Circle the correct answer to each question below. Underline the sentence in the selection where the answer is found.

1. How much did Rosa Parks pay in fines and court costs?
   a. $23
   b. $4
   c. $10
   d. $14

2. Which lawyer won the *Brown* decision?
   a. Thurgood Marshall
   b. Dr. Martin Luther King Jr.
   c. Medgar Evers
   d. John Lewis

3. Who led the Mississippi Freedom Democratic Party?
   a. Rosa Parks
   b. John Lewis
   c. Fannie Lou Hamer
   d. Medgar Evers

4. When was Medgar Evers murdered?
   a. September 2, 1957
   b. February 1, 1960
   c. December 1, 1955
   d. June 12, 1963

5. What did the Little Rock Nine try to integrate?
   a. lunch counters
   b. interstate buses
   c. a high school
   d. a law school

6. Which of these people tried to desegregate a lunch counter?
   a. Elizabeth Eckford
   b. James Meredith
   c. Ezell Blair Jr.
   d. Ruby Bridges

7. Which minister organized boycotts in Montgomery and marches in Selma?
   a. Rosa Parks
   b. Medgar Evers
   c. Ralph Abernathy
   d. James Meredith

8. Which of these was not a member of the Little Rock Nine?
   a. David Richmond
   b. Jefferson Thomas
   c. Melba Pattillo
   d. Carlotta Walls

9. How did most African Americans boycotting Montgomery buses get to work?
   a. They changed jobs.
   b. They took the train.
   c. They walked.
   d. all of the above

10. How did officials try to keep Fannie Lou Hamer from voting in Mississippi?
    a. literacy test
    b. poll tax
    c. paying her money
    d. both a and b

Teacher Lesson Plans for Language Arts

Poetry

Objective: Students will develop skills in reading and understanding poetry.

Materials: copies of African American Poets (page 46); Reading Songs as Poetry in Two Voices (pages 47–50); copies of poems listed on page 46 (available in books and on the Internet)

Procedure

1. Reproduce and distribute Reading Songs as Poetry in Two Voices (page 47). Have students review the vocabulary and rhyme in the song.

2. Review the nature of poetry in two voices, stressing the importance of timing so that the two voices work in unison. You may wish to assign this activity to two capable students and have them demonstrate how to present a poem.

3. Reproduce and distribute Reading Songs as Poetry in Two Voices (pages 48–50). Have each pair of students choose a song listed on these pages or assign them. Tell students to choose their parts, and allow them to practice for several days before presenting their poems to the class. Help them with unfamiliar words and terms.

4. Reproduce and distribute African American Poets (page 46). Offer books of poems by these and other African American poets and/or Internet access to the poems. Encourage each pair of students to choose a poem, divide it into two voices and a chorus, and present it to the class.

Assessment: Have students present their poems to the entire class. Base performance assessments on pacing, volume, expression, and focus of the participants.

Public Speaking and Oral Language

Objective: Students will develop skills in oral presentation techniques.

Materials: copies of Public Speaking (page 51), Becoming a Public Speaker (page 52), Focus on an Orator: Frederick Douglass (page 53), "The Meaning of July Fourth for the Negro" (page 54), Focus on an Orator: Sojourner Truth (page 55), and "Ain't I a Woman?" (page 56), Famous Speeches by African Americans (page 57); additional reading selections from books, encyclopedias, and Internet sources for enrichment

Procedure

1. Reproduce and distribute the pages listed above. Review the choices for styles of public speaking. Review the preparation steps and Tips for Success given on page 52.

2. Have students read Focus on an Orator: Frederick Douglass and Focus on an Orator: Sojourner Truth. They can also read the speeches of both orators.

3. Encourage students to select one of these speeches or a portion of one of the speeches listed on page 57 to learn and present to the class. Students can find copies on the Internet or in books of African American speeches.

4. Instruct students to prepare their speeches. Schedule each student to present so that only two or three speeches are given at any one time.

Assessment: Assess students by using the Tips for Success guide on page 52. Encourage all students to positively critique their own presentations and others.

Teacher Lesson Plans for Language Arts *(cont.)*

=========================== **Persuasive Speech** ===========================

Objective: Students will learn to write and deliver a persuasive speech.

Materials: copies of Write Your Own Persuasive Speech (pages 58–59); news sources

Procedure

1. Reproduce and distribute copies of Write Your Own Persuasive Speech. Read both pages with students so that they have a sense of purpose.
2. Provide time, direction, and news sources so that students can discuss issues in American life. Have students brainstorm suggested topics for their speeches and then choose the best one.
3. Review the concepts of argument and counter-argument.
4. Stress the importance of a good lead sentence and introduction, as well as a strong concluding paragraph.
5. Schedule time during the week for students to create first drafts and revisions of their speeches.
6. Encourage students to practice their speeches at home, outdoors alone, or in groups at school.
7. Schedule presentations to the class over several days.

Assessment: Assess students on the written quality of their speeches and their oral presentations.

=============================== **Literature** ===============================

Objective: Students will read from and respond to literature in the form of novellas and novels.

Materials: copies of Focus on an Author: Mildred D. Taylor (page 60), Working with Novellas (page 61), Focus on an Author: Christopher Paul Curtis (page 62), Read and Respond: *The Watsons Go to Birmingham—1963* (page 63), Read and Respond: *Bud, Not Buddy* (page 64), and Read and Respond: *Elijah of Buxton* (page 65); copies of books listed above and *The Gold Cadillac, The Friendship, Mississippi Bridge, Song of the Trees, The Well: David's Story,* and a few of Taylor's novels, such as *Roll of Thunder, Hear My Cry* and *The Land*

Procedure

1. Reproduce and distribute Focus on an Author: Mildred D. Taylor and Working with Novellas. Read and discuss the information about the author. Assign one of the listed novellas by the author to a small group or the class. Tell students to read the novella and complete the Elements of Literature outline on page 61. Encourage students to share their information and discuss the novellas with their groups or the class.
2. Reproduce and distribute Focus on the Author: Christopher Paul Curtis. Assign the three books and distribute the appropriate pages based on the book assignments: Read and Respond: *The Watsons Go to Birmingham—1963*, Read and Respond: *Bud, Not Buddy*, and Read and Respond: *Elijah of Buxton*.
3. Instruct students to read their Read and Respond pages and then read the novels. Have them meet in small groups to discuss each book separately using the Read and Respond pages as guidelines. You might have one meeting with all of the students reading these novels to discuss overlapping themes, tones, time periods, etc.

Assessment: Assess students on their understanding of the novels, their discussions, and the quality of their questions and answers.

| 1500 | 1550 | 1600 | 1650 | 1700 | 1750 | 1800 | 1850 | 1900 | 1950 | 2000 |

Teacher Lesson Plans for Language Arts *(cont.)*

Readers' Theater

Objective: Students will learn to use their voices effectively in dramatic reading.

Materials: copies of Readers' Theater Notes (page 66), Background Information: George Washington Carver (page 67), Readers' Theater: We Don't Take Negroes Here (pages 68–70), and Readers' Theater Discussion (page 71); additional reading selections from books, encyclopedias, and Internet sources for enrichment

Procedure

1. Reproduce and distribute Readers' Theater Notes and Background Information: George Washington Carver. Review the basic concepts of Readers' Theater with the class. Read and review the background information about George Washington Carver.

2. Reproduce and distribute We Don't Take Negroes Here. Put students in small groups, and allow time over several days for them to practice reading the script together.

3. Schedule class performances, and have students present the prepared script.

4. Reproduce and distribute Readers' Theater Discussion. Moderate the discussion, and encourage students to write their own Readers' Theater using a person or topic in their African American Studies, as suggested on page 66.

5. Schedule classroom performances of these scripts, or invite another class to view the production.

Assessment: Base performance assessments on pacing, volume, expression, and focus of the participants. Student-created scripts should demonstrate general writing skills, dramatic tension, and a good plot.

African American Poets

Poets use their poetic voices to paint word pictures of their lives and the lives of other people.

Maya Angelou

Maya Angelou is both a poet and an actor. Her writing is expressive of her ability to adjust to painful events in her life. Her books of poems include *Just Give Me a Cool Drink of Water . . . 'fore I Diiie*, *I Know Why the Caged Bird Sings*, *I Shall Not Be Moved*, and *Life Doesn't Frighten Me*, a book of poems for children. She recited her poem "On the Pulse of Morning" at the inauguration of President Clinton.

Paul Dunbar

Paul Dunbar was a popular African American poet of the 1890s and early 20th century who expressed his personal hopes and dreams in lines that appealed to many readers. A friend of the Wright brothers and an associate of Frederick Douglass, Dunbar relished in reciting his poetry publicly. Dunbar's poetry often caught the flavor of African American country life, love lost and found, and the subtleties of life for an African American.

His books of poetry include *Oak and Ivy*, *Poems of Cabin and Field*, *Lyrics of Sunshine and Shadow,* and *L'il' Gal*.

Langston Hughes

Langston Hughes was a major figure in the Harlem Renaissance, a period in the early 20th century when the work of African American writers flowered. The poetry of Langston Hughes expresses the flavor of African American life and the feelings of his people. Some of his poems, especially those in his first book, *The Weary Blues*, have a style similar to the blues and jazz style of the 1920s. One of his most famous poems is "The Negro Speaks of Rivers," a poem expressing the many rivers and places that African Americans have lived over human history. Other poems include "Harlem Night Song," "As Befits a Man," and "Late Last Night."

Assignment

1. Use the library or Internet to find a poem you like written by these or other African American poets.

2. Practice reading the poem aloud with a classmate. Get a feel for the force and flow of the language.

3. Read the poem to the class.

Reading Songs as Poetry in Two Voices

Reading poetry as songs in two voices is an enjoyable experience for the presenters and the listeners. Each of the songs on this page and the following pages have been arranged for two speakers, with the chorus read by both speakers together.

Assignment

1. Read the introduction for the song/poem.
2. Silently read the song as a poem several times.
3. Choose a partner.
4. Decide who will be the first and who will be the second speaker. Read the chorus parts together.
5. Practice reading your song/poem aloud several times over the course of several days.
6. Present your reading to the class and in other classrooms.

Special Notes

- You may choose to do the entire song/poem as a chorus with both partners saying all the lines together.
- You may choose to sing the songs if you wish.
- You may wish to change or add lines to the songs as the civil rights marchers of the 20th century often did.

This old song invokes undying strength of character and determination.

First Speaker:	"We Shall Not Be Moved"
Chorus:	We shall not
	We shall not be moved
	We shall not
	We shall not be moved
Second Speaker:	Just like a tree that's planted by the water
	We shall not be moved
Chorus:	We shall not
	We shall not be moved
	We shall not
	We shall not be moved
First Speaker:	Black and white together,
	We shall not be moved
Chorus:	We shall not
	We shall not be moved
	We shall not
	We shall not be moved
Second Speaker:	Just like a tree that's standing by the water
	We shall not be moved

Reading Songs as Poetry in Two Voices *(cont.)*

The song below goes back to the days of slavery. Singing the song was certain to bring severe punishment (such as a whipping or removal of the tongue) or death to anyone caught singing it, even in church. It may have been first sung publicly when the Union army under General Sherman marched through Georgia in 1864. Various versions of the song were sung during the civil rights movement in the 1950s and 1960s.

First Speaker:	"Oh, Freedom (The Freedom Song)"
Chorus:	Oh, freedom
	Oh, freedom
	Oh, freedom
	Over me
Second Speaker:	And before I'll be a slave
	I'll be buried in my grave
	And go home to my Lord and be free.
Chorus:	No more weeping
	No more weeping
	No more weeping
	Over me
First Speaker:	And before I'll be a slave
	I'll be buried in my grave
	And go home to my Lord and be free.
Chorus:	There'll be singin'
	There'll be singin'
	There'll be singin'
	Over me
Second Speaker:	And before I'll be a slave
	I'll be buried in my grave
	And go home to my Lord and be free

Create Your Own Version

During the civil rights movement, many protesters substituted the words "No more segregation" or "No more discrimination" in the "No more weeping" lines. Substitute these lines with your own words, and create your own version of the song on a separate sheet of paper.

Reading Songs as Poetry in Two Voices *(cont.)*

The song below was in many ways the anthem of the civil rights movement in the middle of the 20th century. Various versions of the song were heard in many marches, sit-ins, and protest activities. Like many other freedom songs, it came from a spiritual sung in African American churches for generations.

First Speaker:	"We Shall Overcome"
Second Speaker:	We shall overcome
	We shall overcome
	We shall overcome some day
Chorus:	Oh, deep in my heart
	I do believe
	We shall overcome some day
First Speaker:	We'll walk hand in hand
	We'll walk hand in hand
	We'll walk hand in hand some day
Chorus:	Oh, deep in my heart
	I do believe
	We shall overcome some day
Second Speaker:	We shall all be free
	We shall all be free
	We shall all be free some day
Chorus:	Oh, deep in my heart
	I do believe
	We shall overcome some day

Try This

Create your own version of this marching song, substituting and adding words to fit the general rhythm. You might try such lines as "All Americans," "All colors," "All people," "We shall live together," or "We shall be one."

Your verses: _____

_____

_____

_____

_____

Reading Songs as Poetry in Two Voices *(cont.)*

This old song based on religious faith had many versions and was often sung on long marches and civil rights protests.

First Speaker: "Ain't Gonna Let Nobody Turn Me Around"

Second Speaker: Ain't gonna let nobody turn me around

Turn me around, turn me around

Ain't gonna let nobody turn me around

Chorus: I'm gonna keep on a'walkin, keep on a'talkin

Marchin' down to freedom land

First Speaker: Ain't gonna let segregation turn me around

Turn me around, turn me around

Ain't gonna let segregation turn me around

Chorus: I'm gonna keep on a'walkin, keep on a'talkin

Marchin' up to freedom's land

Second Speaker: Ain't gonna let no Jim Crow turn me around

Turn me around, turn me around

Ain't gonna let no Jim Crow turn me around

Chorus: I'm gonna keep on a'walkin, keep on a'talkin

Marchin' up to freedom's land

First Speaker: Ain't gonna let injustice turn me around

Turn me around, turn me around

Ain't gonna let injustice turn me around

Chorus: I'm gonna keep on a'walkin, keep on a'talkin

Marchin' up to freedom's land

Second Speaker: Ain't gonna let nobody turn me around

Turn me around, turn me around

Ain't gonna let nobody turn me around

Chorus: I'm gonna keep on a'walkin, keep on a'talkin

Gonna build a brand new world

1500 1550 1600 1650 1700 1750 1800 1850 1900 1950 2000

Public Speaking

Famous African American Orators

African Americans overcame prejudice and had their concerns heard because many of their leaders were impassioned and dynamic public speakers. Earlier orators, such as Frederick Douglass and Sojourner Truth, became leaders in the antislavery movement and were vital participants in the campaign to abolish slavery.

Ida B. Wells, W. E. B. Du Bois, and Mary C. Terrell spoke against the harsh injustices and mistreatment of African Americans in the years after the Civil War. Shirley Chisholm, Barbara Jordan, and many others spoke eloquently during the civil rights movement of the 1950s and 1960s. One of the most eloquent speakers was Reverend Martin Luther King Jr.

Choosing a Style

On these pages, you will acquire skills in delivering a speech, originally given by someone else, and also in creating your own speeches.

- You may choose to deliver a speech first given by a famous leader, such as the speeches by Frederick Douglass or Sojourner Truth on the following pages.

- You may write your own persuasive speech using the outline on pages 58 and 59.

- You may create an impromptu speech that is delivered from an outline or notes.

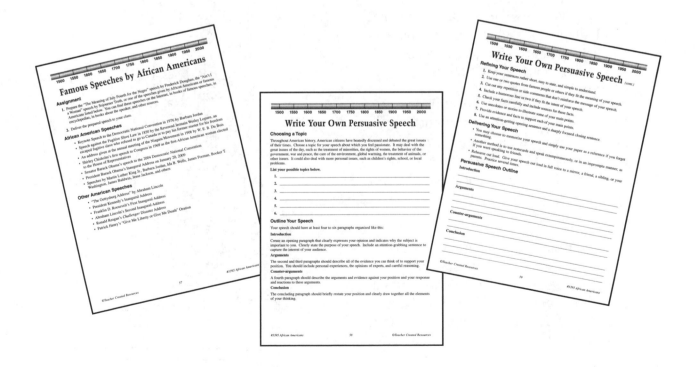

Becoming a Public Speaker

Preparing to Read a Speech by a Famous Person

1. Read through the speech several times.

2. Get a feel for the force and flow of the language.

3. Express the meaning and intent of the speech in one or two sentences.

4. Underline the words or sentences that should be delivered with force or special emphasis.

5. Memorize the speech or know it well enough so that you rarely have to glance at the script.

Tips for Success

- Dress formally. Wear neat clothes or dress clothes.

- Maintain good posture. Stand straight. Balance yourself using both of your feet. Don't lock your knees. Relax your body. Tell yourself to be comfortable.

- Center your mind. Don't get distracted.

- Establish eye contact. Look at various persons in the audience who are paying good attention to what you are saying— teachers, parents, serious students, and people you don't know.

- Speak loudly. Be conversational at times. Speak more forcefully on important points. Never shout, but always be loud enough to hear. Vary your tone of voice to match the mood and feeling of what you are saying. Don't drop your voice at the end of sentences or paragraphs.

- Breathe from your diaphragm. (The diaphragm is the large muscle at the bottom of your rib cage that allows you to control your breathing.) Take deep breaths between paragraphs and important points, but don't be obvious about it.

- Speak slowly and clearly. Speak a little slower than normal speech patterns. Don't race to finish your speech.

Focus on an Orator: Frederick Douglass

Frederick Douglass was born a slave in Tuckahoe, Maryland, on February 1818. The son of a slave woman and her white owner, Douglass was raised by his grandmother until he was eight years old. He only saw his mother a few times in his lifetime because she lived on a different plantation. At the age of eight, he was given to the Auld family, who lived in Baltimore. The family gave him better clothes and food, and the mother taught him to read until her husband stopped the practice. It was illegal to teach slaves to read in many slave states. Douglass continued to teach himself to read from newspapers.

At the age of fifteen, he was sent away to a plantation where he worked in the fields for a brutal "slavebreaker" named Edward Covey. Here, he witnessed and experienced the brutal reality of slavery. He was frequently whipped and left hungry and cold. He fought with the overseer and eventually ran away or "stole himself," as he later described his escape. A friend, Anna Murray, made him a sailor suit and helped him escape. He reached New York City in 1838 where he married Anna. Friends raised money to help him buy his freedom from his owner. It cost $711.66, a sum worth at least ten times as much in today's currency.

Douglass started giving dynamic speeches at abolitionist meetings. He also attended and spoke at anti-slavery conventions. One of Douglass's most famous speeches was given at an event celebrating the signing of the Declaration of Independence. During this address, he said, "This Fourth of July is *yours*, not *mine*. You may rejoice, I must mourn."

In Douglass's lifetime, he wrote three autobiographies, but his most famous one was written in 1841, *Narrative of the Life of Frederick Douglass, An American Slave.* He started three different newspapers advocating the emancipation of slaves. Douglass was a friend and trusted advisor of President Lincoln. He strongly advocated allowing African Americans to fight in the Civil War. In 1877, he became a U.S. Marshal for the District of Columbia. Douglass died in 1895 at his home in Washington, D.C.

"The Meaning of July Fourth for the Negro"

The text below contains selections from the famous speech by Frederick Douglass. It was delivered at Corinthian Hall in Rochester, New York, on July 5, 1852.

Fellow Citizens, I am not wanting in respect for the fathers of this republic. The signers of the Declaration of Independence were brave men. They were great men, too—great enough to give frame to a great age. . . . The point from which I am compelled to view them is not, certainly, the most favorable; and yet I cannot contemplate their great deeds with less than admiration. They were statesmen, patriots and heroes, and for the good they did, and the principles they contended for, I will unite with you to honor their memory. . . .

Fellow-citizens, pardon me, allow me to ask, why am I called upon to speak here to-day? What have I, or those I represent, to do with your national independence? Are the great principles of political freedom and of natural justice, embodied in that Declaration of Independence, extended to us? And am I, therefore, called upon to bring our humble offering to the national altar, and to confess the benefits and express devout gratitude for the blessings resulting from your independence to us?

Would to God, both for your sakes and ours, that an affirmative answer could be truthfully returned to these questions! Then would my task be light, and my burden easy and delightful. . . .

But such is not the state of the case. I say it with a sad sense of the disparity between us. I am not included within the pale of glorious anniversary! . . . The rich inheritance of justice, liberty, prosperity and independence, bequeathed by your fathers, is shared by you, not by me. The sunlight that brought light and healing to you, has brought stripes and death to me. This Fourth July is yours, not mine. You may rejoice, I must mourn. . . . Do you mean, citizens, to mock me, by asking me to speak to-day? . . .

Fellow-citizens, above your national, tumultuous joy, I hear the mournful wail of millions whose chains, heavy and grievous yesterday, are, to-day, rendered more intolerable by the jubilee shouts that reach them. . . . My subject, then, fellow-citizens, is American slavery. I shall see this day and its popular characteristics from the slave's point of view. . . .

What, to the American slave, is your 4th of July? I answer: a day that reveals to him, more than all other days in the year, the gross injustice and cruelty to which he is the constant victim. To him, your celebration is a sham; your boasted liberty, an unholy license; your national greatness, swelling vanity; your sounds of rejoicing are empty and heartless; your shouts of liberty and equality, hollow mockery. . . . There is not a nation on the earth guilty of practices more shocking and bloody than are the people of the United States, at this very hour. . . .

Allow me to say, in conclusion, notwithstanding the dark picture I have this day presented, of the state of the nation, I do not despair of this country. . . . I, therefore, leave off where I began, with hope. While drawing encouragement from "the Declaration of Independence," the great principles it contains, and the genius of American Institutions, my spirit is also cheered by the obvious tendencies of the age. Nations do not now stand in the same relation to each other that they did ages ago. . . . Walled cities and empires have become unfashionable. . . . Intelligence is penetrating the darkest corners of the globe. It makes its pathway over and under the sea, as well as on the earth. . . . Oceans no longer divide, but link nations together. . . .

In the fervent aspirations of William Lloyd Garrison, I say, and let every heart join in saying it:

> *God speed the hour, the glorious hour,*
> *When none on earth*
> *Shall exercise a lordly power,*
> *Nor in a tyrant's presence cower;*
> *But to all manhood's stature tower,*
> *By equal birth!*
> *That hour will come, to each, to all,*
> *And from his Prison-house, to thrall*
> *Go forth.*
>
> *Until that year, day, hour, arrive,*
> *With head, and heart, and hand I'll strive,*
> *To break the rod, and rend the gyve,*
> *The spoiler of his prey deprive—*
> *So witness Heaven!*
> *And never from my chosen post,*
> *Whate'er the peril or the cost,*
> *Be driven.*

Focus on an Orator: Sojourner Truth

"Children, I talk to God, and God talks to me." Sojourner Truth often began her remarkable speeches with these words. She was an electrifying orator who thrilled audiences with her message and presence as she lectured throughout the North during the years preceding the Civil War.

Sojourner Truth was a former slave who escaped in 1826 and who began her crusade for the abolition of slavery and the rights of women in 1841. She could neither read nor write, and many advocates of women's suffrage were afraid she would hurt the women's rights movement. Her "Ain't I a Woman" speech—similar to those she gave over many years—at the Ohio Women's Rights Convention in 1851 earned her the respect of most of the suffrage leaders.

Sojourner started life as a Dutch-speaking slave named Isabella in New York State. She watched her twelve brothers and sisters be sold at different times, and Isabella was sold as a teenager to John Dumont who chose her slave husband for her when she was seventeen years old. They had five children.

Isabella was entitled to freedom in ten years due to the New York Emancipation Act that took effect in 1827. Dumont promised to free her a year early if she worked hard for him for nine years. She fulfilled her part of the bargain, but he refused to let her go. Isabella ran away with her baby, Sophia. A Quaker family bought her and her baby and then freed them. She discovered that her five-year-old son, Peter, had been sold to Alabama planters against New York State law. She sued Dumont and won her case, becoming the first African American woman in America to win a lawsuit against a white man.

She adopted the name Sojourner Truth in 1843 when she followed voices in her head that told her to become a traveling preacher. She spoke about religion in parts of New York, Connecticut, and Massachusetts. Sojourner became a powerful voice for God's love, despite the fact that she could neither read nor write. She soon became a strong voice for the abolition of slavery and the rights of women. Sojourner (which means *traveler*) journeyed through the western states, including Ohio, Kansas, and Indiana, delivering her unique message. *The Narrative of Sojourner Truth* was written by a friend and widely read. She met President Lincoln in the White House in 1864 and tried to help freed African Americans after the war.

"Ain't I a Woman?"

The speech below is a version of the one Sojourner Truth gave to the Ohio Women's Rights Convention in 1851.

Well, children, where there is so much racket there must be something out of kilter. I think that 'twixt the negroes of the South and the women at the North, all talking about rights, the white men will be in a fix pretty soon. But what's all this here talking about?

That man over there says that women need to be helped into carriages, and lifted over ditches, and to have the best place everywhere. Nobody ever helps me into carriages, or over mud puddles, or gives me any best place! And ain't I a woman? Look at me! Look at my arm! I have plowed and planted, and gathered into barns, and no man could head me! And ain't I a woman? I could work as much and eat as much as a man—when I could get it—and bear the lash, as well! And ain't I a woman? I have borne thirteen children, and seen most sold off to slavery, and when I cried out with my mother's grief, none but Jesus heard me! And ain't I a woman?

Then they talk about this thing in the head; what's this they call it? [Intellect.] That's it, honey. What's that got to do with women's rights or negroes' rights? If my cup won't hold but a pint, and yours holds a quart, wouldn't you be mean not to let me have my little half-measure full?

Then that little man in black there, he says women can't have as much rights as men, 'cause Christ wasn't a woman! Where did your Christ come from? Where did your Christ come from? From God and a woman! Man had nothing to do with Him.

If the first woman God ever made was strong enough to turn the world upside down all alone, these women together ought to be able to turn it back, and get it right side up again! And now they is asking to do it, the men better let them.

Obliged to you for hearing me, and now old Sojourner ain't got nothing more to say.

| 1500 | 1550 | 1600 | 1650 | 1700 | 1750 | 1800 | 1850 | 1900 | 1950 | 2000 |

Famous Speeches by African Americans

Assignment

1. Prepare the "The Meaning of July Fourth for the Negro" speech by Frederick Douglass, the "Ain't I a Woman" speech by Sojourner Truth, or one of the speeches given by African Americans or famous Americans listed below. You can find these speeches on the Internet, in books of famous speeches, in encyclopedias, in books about the speaker, and other sources.

2. Deliver the prepared speech to your class.

African American Speeches

- Keynote Speech to the Democratic National Convention in 1976 by Barbara Jordan
- Speech against the Fugitive Slave Law in 1850 by the Reverend Jermain Wesley Loguen, an escaped fugitive slave who refused to go to Canada or to pay his former master for his freedom
- An address given at the annual meeting of the Niagara Movement in 1906 by W. E. B. Du Bois
- Shirley Chisholm's first speech to Congress in 1969 as the first African American woman elected to the House of Representatives
- Senator Barack Obama's speech to the 2004 Democratic National Convention
- President Barack Obama's Inaugural Address on January 20, 2009
- Speeches by Martin Luther King Jr., Barbara Jordan, Ida B. Wells, James Forman, Booker T. Washington, James Baldwin, Jesse Jackson, and others

Other American Speeches

- "The Gettysburg Address" by Abraham Lincoln
- President Kennedy's Inaugural Address
- Franklin D. Roosevelt's First Inaugural Address
- Abraham Lincoln's Second Inaugural Address
- Ronald Reagan's *Challenger* Disaster Address
- Patrick Henry's "Give Me Liberty or Give Me Death" Oration

Write Your Own Persuasive Speech

Choosing a Topic

Throughout American history, American citizens have heatedly discussed and debated the great issues of their times. Choose a topic for your speech about which you feel passionate. It may deal with the great issues of the day, such as the treatment of minorities, the rights of women, the behavior of the government, war and peace, the care of the environment, global warming, the treatment of animals, or other issues. It could also deal with more personal issues, such as children's rights, school, or local problems.

List your possible topics below.

1. _____
2. _____
3. _____
4. _____
5. _____
6. _____

Outline Your Speech

Your speech should have at least four to six paragraphs organized like this:

Introduction

Create an opening paragraph that clearly expresses your opinion and indicates why the subject is important to you. Clearly state the purpose of your speech. Include an attention-grabbing sentence to capture the interest of your audience.

Arguments

The second and third paragraphs should describe all of the evidence you can think of to support your position. You should include personal experiences, the opinions of experts, and careful reasoning.

Counter-arguments

A fourth paragraph should describe the arguments and evidence against your position and your response and reactions to these arguments.

Conclusion

The concluding paragraph should briefly restate your position and clearly draw together all the elements of your thinking.

Write Your Own Persuasive Speech *(cont.)*

Refining Your Speech

1. Keep your sentences rather short, easy to state, and simple to understand.

2. Use one or two quotes from famous people or others if they fit the meaning of your speech.

3. Cut out any repetition or side comments that don't reinforce the message of your speech.

4. Include a humorous line or two if they fit the intent of your speech.

5. Check your facts carefully and include sources for these facts.

6. Use anecdotes or stories to illustrate some of your main points.

7. Provide evidence and facts to support each of your main points.

8. Use an attention-getting opening sentence and a sharply focused closing sentence.

Delivering Your Speech

- You may choose to memorize your speech and simply use your paper as a reference if you forget something.

- Another method is to use notecards and speak extemporaneously, or in an impromptu manner, as if you were speaking to friends.

- Rehearse out loud. Give your speech out loud in full voice to a mirror, a friend, a sibling, or your parents. Practice several times.

Persuasive Speech Outline

Introduction

_____

_____

Arguments

_____

_____

_____

Counter-arguments

_____

_____

Conclusion

_____

_____

_____

Focus on an Author: Mildred D. Taylor

Mildred D. Taylor became an author, in part, to correct some of the racial stereotypes and historical inaccuracies she encountered as a student. She believed that the school textbooks she read as a student in the 1950s diminished the achievements of African Americans and did not truly portray the mistreatment of African Americans during the years of slavery or during the long period of second-class citizenship imposed after the Civil War. Taylor was deeply influenced by her storyteller father, who often recounted the history of her family in the post-Civil War decades.

Novelist

Taylor created the saga of the Logan family in *Roll of Thunder, Hear My Cry* as a way to describe how African Americans struggled against the injustices and second-class citizenship of the Reconstruction period and Jim Crow laws. The author received the Newbery Award in 1977 for this book, which was her first story set in Depression-era Mississippi. The Logan children (Cassie, Stacey, Christopher-John, and Little Man) can't ride on a school bus for white children, must use discarded textbooks from white schools, and are helpless to stop the near-lynching of a classmate. Even though they are subjected to routine humiliation by the dominant white culture, the family members don't quit. They simply stiffen their resolve to survive.

Other novels that highlight this family are the sequels *Let the Circle Be Unbroken* and *The Road to Memphis*, which continue the story with Cassie's efforts to attain a college education during World War II. The prequel is entitled *The Land*. Set immediately after the Civil War, *The Land* tells how Cassie's grandfather, Paul-Edward Logan, son of a white owner and a slave woman, came to acquire the land that the family has held onto for generations.

Novellas

Four of Taylor's five novellas also feature the Logan family: *Mississippi Bridge, The Friendship, Song of the Trees*, and *The Well: David's Story*. They reflect the real-life experiences of African American children growing up in Mississippi in the first decades of the 1900s. The fifth novella, *The Gold Cadillac*, is based on the author's own vacation experiences with segregation and discrimination in the 1950s.

| 1500 | 1550 | 1600 | 1650 | 1700 | 1750 | 1800 | 1850 | 1900 | 1950 | 2000 |

Working with Novellas

A novella is longer and more detailed than a short story and much shorter than a full-length novel. A novella usually has a single plot line and a few sharply detailed characters facing one problem or conflict.

Assignment

1. Read one of the Mildred Taylor novellas listed on page 60.
2. Complete the Elements of Literature outline below.

Elements of Literature: A Novella

Genre (historical fiction, fantasy, contemporary realism, etc.)

_____

Setting of the novella (Where and when does the story take place?)

_____

Characters (Name the main and supporting characters of the story.)

_____

_____

Point of View (What kind of narrator tells the story, first person or third person?)

_____

Plot (Tell the crucial events of the novella.)

_____

_____

Problem/Conflict (Describe the basic problem or conflict in the novella for the main character.)

_____

_____

Climax (What one event in the novel does everything lead up to and then lead to a resolution?)

_____

_____

Resolution (How does the novella end—for the main character, especially?)

_____

_____

Feeling/Tone (What is the general tone of the book—depressing, uplifting, light? Choose the appropriate descriptive words.)

_____

Theme(s) (What message(s) about the meaning of life does the author want to communicate to the reader?)

Focus on an Author: Christopher Paul Curtis

Christopher Paul Curtis has written three major historical novels for children. *Bud, Not Buddy* received the Newbery medal as the best children's book of 2000, while *The Watsons Go to Birmingham—1963* and *Elijah of Buxton* each received Newbery Honor status as exceptional books in the years in which they were written.

The Watsons Go to Birmingham—1963 was the author's first novel. The story opens in Flint, Michigan, where the narrator, ten-year-old Kenny, endures a great deal of discomfort from his older brother, Byron. Kenny has many fears to face, including his brother's frequent taunting, harassment, and sometimes crazy antics. The parents hope that the influence of Mrs. Watson's mother, Grandma Sands, will be a strict and effective cure for Byron's behavior. The family travels from Flint to Grandma Sands's home in Birmingham, Alabama, in an old car called the Brown Bomber. The parents prepare for travel through the South with all of the segregated facilities and potential police harassment. While in Birmingham, the bombing of the Sixteenth Avenue Baptist Church occurs with the loss of four young girls' lives. This profoundly affects Kenny.

Bud, Not Buddy is set in Depression-era Michigan. The narrator and main character of this book is ten-year-old Bud Caldwell, an orphan who leaves his cruel foster parents and goes on the road looking for his father. His mother is dead, and all he has is a poster featuring a jazz musician who Bud believes to be his father. In the course of his travels, he meets kind families in a breadline and a Depression Hooverville until he finds a family of his own.

Elijah of Buxton is set in the years just before the Civil War in the Canadian settlement of Buxton, a place settled by escaped slaves and their families who had to leave the United States in order to avoid the Fugitive Slave Law, which required runaway slaves to be returned to their owners. The main character is a school-age boy who narrates a story of hope and courage in the face of treachery and cruelty.

The author worked on the General Motors factory line for many years, as did his father, before becoming a professional writer. Some of the details in his stories, like the jazz band in *Bud, Not Buddy,* are based on his own family's experiences. All of his books contain several humorous situations, and all reflect the condition of African Americans in the context of the times the stories are set.

Read and Respond:
The Watsons Go to Birmingham—1963

Assignment

1. Read *The Watsons Go to Birmingham—1963.*
2. Answer the questions below, and share your responses in a small-group or class discussion.

Discussion Starters

1. Why is Kenny embarrassed to read in the sixth grade? Would you be embarrassed in the same situation?
2. Why are Rufus and Cody looked down upon by many of the children in school? Where are they from? What is different about their speech patterns?
3. How do Kenny and his parents help Rufus and Cody?
4. What are the funniest things that happen in the book—especially with Byron?
5. Describe two or three good things that Byron does as Kenny's big brother.
6. How does the bombing in Birmingham affect Kenny?
7. How has Grandma Sands changed in the mind of Mrs. Watson?
8. What special preparations did the Watsons have to make for traveling through the South in 1963?

Your Discussion Starters

Write three Discussion Starters to share with the class or a small group.

1. _____
2. _____
3. _____

Passages to Share

Choose three passages to share with the class or your group. Explain your reason for sharing each passage.

1. Page _____ Reason_____
2. Page _____ Reason_____
3. Page _____ Reason_____

Dedication

Who is the book dedicated to and why?

_____

_____

Read and Respond: *Bud, Not Buddy*

Assignment

1. Read *Bud, Not Buddy*.
2. Answer the questions below, and share your responses in a small-group or class discussion.

Discussion Starters

1. Should Bud have left the foster home? Explain your answer.
2. Why does the family in the breakfast breadline pretend that Bud is their child?
3. How are homeless people, like Bud and the others living in the Hooverville, treated during the Depression?
4. Name three instances where people he doesn't know are kind to Bud. Who do you think is the kindest person or family to help Bud? Explain your answer.
5. Are the people who mistreat Bud prejudiced against him because he is poor or because he is African American? Explain your answer.
6. Should the police have burned down the Hooverville? Use examples from the story to explain your answer.
7. Why do some men choose to join unions and others oppose them? Should the men join unions? Explain your answer.
8. Why doesn't Herman E. Calloway accept Bud at first?
9. Which member of the band do you like best? Explain your answer.
10. How do you know that Bud has musical talent?
11. How is Bud actually related to Herman Calloway?
12. What happens between Mr. Calloway and Bud's mother?

Your Discussion Starters

Write three Discussion Starters to share with the class or your group.

1. _____
2. _____
3. _____

Passages to Share

Choose three passages to share with the class or your group. Explain your reason for sharing each passage.

1. Page _____ Reason_____
2. Page _____ Reason_____
3. Page _____ Reason_____

Which of Bud's Rules and Things did you think were right?

_____

Which one made the most sense to you?

_____

Read and Respond: *Elijah of Buxton*

Assignment

1. Read *Elijah of Buxton*.

2. Answer the questions below, and share your responses in a small-group or class discussion.

Discussion Starters

1. Describe the personality and character of Elijah. Do you like him? Why?

2. What special skills does Elijah possess? What can he do with stones, animals, and tools?

3. How does Elijah help people? Give some examples.

4. Do you trust the preacher? What things does he do in the story that make him appear untrustworthy? What good qualities does the preacher have?

5. What embarrassing things happen to Elijah? Do you sympathize with his embarrassment?

6. How does Elijah free at least one slave?

7. Who do you think will get the baby Elijah brings home—his mother or another woman in the community? Explain your answer.

Understanding Character and Theme

- How does the main character—Elijah—change over time during the course of events in the book? How has he matured, learned about life, and become responsible? Who helped him the most?

- Most well-written books have a theme, or a message about the meaning of life, that the author wants to communicate to the reader. What major theme does the author try to communicate to the readers of *Elijah of Buxton*?

- What other messages about slavery, schooling, family, love, history, personal responsibility, and friendship are communicated in the book?

Learning History

What information can you learn in *Elijah of Buxton* about these historical events?

- Fugitive Slave Law

- treatment of slaves in the United States

- Canada's attitude toward slavery and African Americans

- escaping from slavery

- buying a slave's freedom

Learning More

What would you like to learn more about related to this period of American history?

Readers' Theater Notes

Behind the Scenes

Readers' Theater is drama that does not require costumes, props, a stage, or memorization. It is done in the classroom by groups of students who become the cast of the dramatic reading.

Staging

Place four or five stools or chairs in a semicircle at the front of your class or in a separate staging area. Generally, no costumes are used in this type of dramatization, but students dressed in similar clothing or colors can have a nice effect. Simple props can be used but are not required.

Scripting

Each member of your group should have a clearly marked script. Performers should practice several times before presenting the play to the class.

Performing

Performers should enter the classroom quietly and seriously. They should sit silently without moving and wait with their heads lowered. The first reader should begin, and the other readers should focus on whoever is reading, except when they are performing.

Assignment

Read the Readers' Theater scripts chosen by your teacher about George Washington Carver. Work with your assigned group to prepare for your performance, and share your interpretation of the script with your class.

Extensions

Write your own Readers' Theater script based on one of these events or another topic related to your study of African Americans. Practice your script with a group of classmates, and then perform it for the rest of the class.

- Rosa Parks refuses to give up her seat on a Montgomery bus.
- A group of freedom riders tries to desegregate buses traveling through the South.
- A group of college students stages a sit-in at a lunch counter.
- Ruby Bridges goes to school in a white New Orleans school.
- The Little Rock Nine face the mobs, police, and troops at Central High.
- Fannie Lou Hamer tries to vote in Mississippi.
- A group of friends attend the March on Washington.
- An African American family travels into the South during the 1950s.

Background Information: George Washington Carver

George Washington Carver began life as a slave on the farm of Moses Carver in the Ozarks region of Missouri. Bandits kidnapped his mother and George when he was still an infant. His mother was never found, but George, a sickly child, and his brother Jim were recovered. When the Civil War ended, slavery was outlawed, and George and his older brother were treated like sons by the Carvers.

Plant Doctor

George was a very bright child who quickly learned how to grow plants, to read, and to paint. As a young boy, he was known in his community as "the plant doctor" and raised his own secret garden in the woods with many varieties of plants. When he became a teenager, George spent several years wandering across Kansas adding to his education. He tried to homestead a farm for a time. After getting a high school degree in Minneapolis, Kansas, George was accepted to and then rejected by Highland University in Kansas because of his race. George was finally accepted by Simpson College and later studied at Iowa State College. He improved his artistic skills and became an expert in the study of hybrid plants, fungi, and other aspects of the science of botany.

Teaching Others

In 1896, Carver accepted a position with Booker T. Washington at Tuskegee Institute in Alabama, a college devoted to offering African Americans a chance to improve their lives. He taught the best practices in agricultural science, as well as botany and biology, and managed an experimental farm. Carver was in charge of the Institute's orchard, beehives, poultry, landscaping, and dairy.

Inventing Uses for Plants

Starting only with a prized microscope given to him by friends in Iowa, Carver used the lab he developed to create many new varieties and uses for plants. He developed a faster-growing cotton plant able to resist an insect called the boll weevil, which destroyed cotton. He taught farmers to rotate crops and improve their land by planting black-eyed peas, which returned nutrients to the soil. He developed more than forty recipes for using these peas. George became the father of chemurgy, the science of finding new uses for products, such as sweet potatoes, peanuts, and even acorns. George invented more than 300 uses for peanuts, including cheese, cream, oils, shampoo, ink, flour, face powder, soap, medicine, and vinegar. He invented about 160 uses for sweet potatoes, including molasses, dye, shoe polish, flour, glue, vinegar, ink, and a kind of rubber.

He refused an offer to work with Thomas Edison and devoted his entire life to the study of nature and the improvement of farming techniques for poor Southern farmers. He died at the age of eighty-three, internationally respected for his achievements and his character.

Readers' Theater: We Don't Take Negroes Here

This script is based on George Washington Carver's first attempt to attend college in Kansas in 1885. There are four speaking parts:

> Brown   Miss Beeler
>
> Carver   Narrator

Narrator: The setting is the inside of President Duncan Brown's office at Highland University in Kansas in 1885. The walls are lined with books. A well-dressed, important-looking man, Duncan Brown, president of the College, is standing behind a large, polished desk. He is looking at a paper and frowning.

Brown: Who are you? What are you doing here?

Carver: I am a new student. My name is George Washington Carver.

Narrator: George Washington Carver hands a letter to Dr. Brown.

Brown: This is ridiculous! It's totally impossible! Where did you get this letter?

Carver: But, sir, I received this letter of acceptance to Highland University from the president of the College, Dr. Duncan Brown.

I sent in all of my records from Minneapolis High School. I had excellent grades and recommendations from the school.

Dr. Brown awarded me a scholarship and instructed me to report today, September 15th.

Brown: I am Dr. Duncan Brown. This is my handwriting. I admit that. But there has been a terrible mistake! This is just not possible!

Your high school record was excellent, and we did award you a scholarship, but we had no idea. We simply cannot accept you at this university.

Carver: But, sir, your letter said . . .

Narrator: Dr. Brown's face twists into a mask of anger. In responding to George, his voice is loud, firm, clear, and as cold as ice.

Brown: We don't take Negroes here.

Carver: But, sir, I worked very hard to prepare myself academically. I took all of the required courses and some special courses to catch up on some deficiencies in math.

Brown: Yes, I can see that you did remarkably well for someone of your race. Your academic record is astonishing. But you didn't inform us on your application that you were a Negro.

Carver: It didn't ask for my race. I hoped it would not matter.

Readers' Theater:
We Don't Take Negroes Here *(cont.)*

Brown: We've never faced this situation before. So far as I know, no Negro has ever applied to Highland University. We have no provisions for dealing with someone of your kind.

It's unthinkable. There'd be no place for you to live. The white students would never permit you to live in the dormitories. The professors would be outraged if you attended their classes. The parents of our students would be scandalized. We simply couldn't allow it.

Carver: But I would find another place to live. I would be unnoticed. I would cause no trouble.

Brown: Why would you, a Negro, want to go to college anyway? You speak well. And you've managed to get through high school. That's exceptional for someone of your race.

Carver: I had hoped to study botany and art. I am very good with plants, and I draw well.

Brown: What would you do with a college education? What job would you get?

It would never do . . . a Negro. . . . You'd be just wasting your time. You'd never get hired after college. It would just be a waste of your time.

Narrator: George seems to shrink for a moment at this rejection and the destruction of his hopes, but he responds slowly and in a dignified voice.

Carver: Time belongs to God. I'm going to college somewhere. There is work for me to do. I must be ready.

Brown: I'm sorry. It is out of the question. We don't take Negroes here. Please leave.

Narrator: George walks out of the office where he meets a white friend and supporter, Miss Beeler, who is waiting for him.

Miss Beeler: They refused to accept you, didn't they?

Carver: Yes. He said that I'd be wasting my time and they didn't accept Negroes.

Miss Beeler: I was afraid this would happen. But you must keep trying. Somewhere, there is a college that will be blind to your color but see the strength of your mind and character.

Carver: I had hoped to study art and how plants grow. I am very skilled at growing things, and I want to become more knowledgeable about plant and animal life. I want to help my people use their new freedom to become successful farmers.

Miss Beeler: George, I just know you'll succeed. You can't let this defeat distract you.

For now, let's forget this unpleasantness and enjoy some music at the church social. Grab your accordion, and let's celebrate the success that you will surely have in the future.

Readers' Theater:
We Don't Take Negroes Here *(cont.)*

Narrator: George Washington Carver did go on to college.

He studied music, art, and other subjects at Simpson College and later studied botany and other sciences at Iowa College.

George Washington Carver later became an important inventor and agricultural scientist. He taught at Tuskegee Institute, where he helped Southern farmers of both races learn how to enrich the soil through the use of better plant selection, composting, and natural fertilizers.

He has had a huge impact on modern farming. He invented hundreds of products made from peanuts, soybeans, and other plants that are also good for the soil.

Readers' Theater Discussion

Assignment

1. Read the Readers' Theater script, "We Don't Take Negroes Here," as well as Background Information: George Washington Carver. You might also want to look at biographies, textbooks, and Internet sources when answering the questions below.

2. Answer the questions, making notes on the lines provided.

3. Share your responses in a small-group or class discussion.

Discussion Starters

1. Why do you think George Washington Carver wanted to go to Highland College?

   _____

   _____

   _____

2. Why do you think so many people in Carver's time were so prejudiced? Do you think it is related to ignorance or hate?

   _____

   _____

   _____

3. What do you think is the most important thing you can learn from Carver's experiences? Explain your answer.

   _____

   _____

   _____

Making It Personal

Given the time he lived in, do you think Carver could or should have done something else when he was rejected at Highland University? Explain your answer.

_____

_____

_____

What do you think was Carver's greatest discovery or invention? Explain your choice.

_____

_____

_____

Teacher Lesson Plans for Social Studies

Using Maps

Objective: Students will learn to use and derive information from maps.

Materials: copies of United States Map in 1850 (pages 74–75) and Understanding Key Places (page 76); reference materials including atlases, almanacs, and other maps

Procedure

1. Reproduce and distribute United States Map in 1850 and Understanding Key Places. Review the information about free and slave states in earlier readings.

2. Review the map on page 75. Use a labeled United States map for reference. Review information about famous African Americans and the states they came from.

3. Have students complete both assignments.

Assessment: Correct the map activity together. Check for understanding and review basic concepts as needed.

Using Timelines

Objective: Students will learn to derive information from a timeline and make timelines relevant to them.

Materials: copies of Timeline of African American Events (pages 77–78); reference materials including books, encyclopedias, texts, atlases, almanacs, and Internet sources

Procedure

1. Collect available resources so that students have plenty of materials from which to find information. Include reading selections from this book.

2. Review the concept of a timeline using the school year as an example.

3. Reproduce and distribute Timeline of African American Events. Review the events listed on the timeline.

4. Instruct students to place additional dates on the timeline as described in the assignment on page 78.

5. Students may want to use the readings from the beginning of the book to locate the ten extra dates for their timelines.

Assessment: Verify the accuracy of the dates and events that students added to the timeline. Assess students' ability to research other events to add to the timeline.

Teacher Lesson Plans for Social Studies *(cont.)*

Researching People and Events

Objective: Students will recognize the significance of African Americans in American History and the events that profoundly affected their lives.

Materials: copies of African American biographies (pages 79–80), African American Heroes and Heroines (page 81), Researching Events (page 82), African American Experiences (page 83), and Become a Famous Person (pages 84–86); reference materials including books, encyclopedias, and Internet sources

Procedure

1. Reproduce and distribute African American Biographies and African American Heroes and Heroines. Review the biographical subjects on page 81, and suggest possible books. Collective biographies (of several people) are listed in the Annotated Bibliography on page 93. Allow students to select the person they want to read about. Encourage students to list events and respond to the discussion starters on page 79.

2. Reproduce and distribute Researching Events and African American Experiences. Have students use reference materials to complete the assignment on page 82 about one of the listed events. Similar sources can be used to research the experiences listed on page 83.

3. Reproduce and distribute Become a Famous Person. Review the research advice on page 84. Indicate the many sources of information you have collected. Discuss the need to take careful notes in preparation for the presentation. Allow students to select their persons from the African American Heroes and Heroines list on page 81 or other famous African Americans or supporters.

4. Give students time to research and prepare their famous person presentations. Arrange a schedule so students can present to the class.

Assessment: Assess African American biographies, events, and experiences on completeness and class discussions.

Assess students on their oral classroom presentations, using the following categories and percentages (or create a rubric of your choosing): general knowledge (50%), dramatic skill (10%), voice (20%), costume (10%), notes (10%).

General Social Studies

Objective: Students will acquire a general understanding of government organization and gain knowledge from living witnesses to history.

Materials: copies of Barack Obama (page 87), Know Your Government (page 88), The Law Matters (page 89), and Collecting Oral Histories (page 90); reference materials including almanacs, encyclopedias, and Internet sources

Procedure

1. Reproduce and distribute Barack Obama, Know Your Government, and The Law Matters. Read and discuss the information about President Obama. Review the worksheets on government organization and the Supreme Court.

2. Reproduce and distribute Collecting Oral Histories. Discuss possible interview subjects in the students' family and neighborhood.

Assessment: Assess students on how complete their information is.

United States Map in 1850

By 1850, The United States was deeply divided between free states in the North (white on the map) and slave states in the South (gray on the map).

Directions: Label each state on the map on page 75. Then list the states under the proper titles.

<table>
<tr><th>Free States</th><th>Slave States</th></tr>
<tr><td>1. _____</td><td>1. _____</td></tr>
<tr><td>2. _____</td><td>2. _____</td></tr>
<tr><td>3. _____</td><td>3. _____</td></tr>
<tr><td>4. _____</td><td>4. _____</td></tr>
<tr><td>5. _____</td><td>5. _____</td></tr>
<tr><td>6. _____</td><td>6. _____</td></tr>
<tr><td>7. _____</td><td>7. _____</td></tr>
<tr><td>8. _____</td><td>8. _____</td></tr>
<tr><td>9. _____</td><td>9. _____</td></tr>
<tr><td>10. _____</td><td>10. _____</td></tr>
<tr><td>11. _____</td><td>11. _____</td></tr>
<tr><td>12. _____</td><td>12. _____</td></tr>
<tr><td>13. _____</td><td>13. _____</td></tr>
<tr><td>14. _____</td><td>14. _____</td></tr>
<tr><td>15. _____</td><td>15. _____</td></tr>
<tr><td>16. _____</td><td></td></tr>
</table>

United States Map in 1850 *(cont.)*

Directions: Label each state below. Then list the states under the proper categories on page 74.

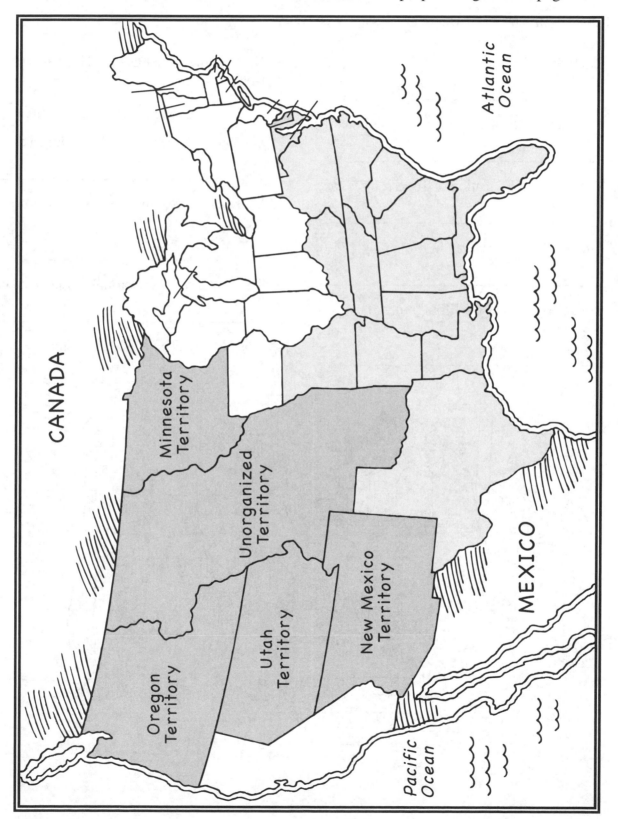

Understanding Key Places

African Americans have followed a path to equality marked by events in many states.

Directions: Name the state where each event occurred.

1. Riots occur in Watts.

   _____

2. The Harlem Renaissance enriches culture.

   _____

3. The Board of Education of Topeka loses case.

   _____

4. Emmett Till is murdered in Money.

   _____

5. Rosa Parks ignites the Montgomery bus boycott.

   _____

6. Nine children enter Central High in Little Rock.

   _____

7. Students in Greensboro sit in at lunch counters.

   _____

8. Dr. King delivers his "I Have a Dream" speech.

   _____

9. The first slaves were brought to Jamestown.

   _____

10. Crispus Attucks is killed in Boston.

   _____

Timeline of African American Events

1539—Esteban the Black guides a Spanish expedition from Mexico through the Southwest searching for seven cities of gold.

1619—The first indentured servants arrive in Jamestown. African slaves arrive soon after.

1770—Crispus Attucks, an African American, dies in the Boston Massacre.

1793—Eli Whitney invents the cotton gin, which makes slavery very profitable in the South.

1820—The Missouri Compromise is passed by Congress to help reduce the conflict over slavery.

1822—The American colony of Liberia is founded in Africa as a self-governing homeland for free blacks.

1827—*Freedom's Journal,* the first African American newspaper, is founded.

1847—Frederick Douglass starts the *North Star,* an abolitionist newspaper.

1849—Harriet Tubman escapes and begins her career as a conductor on the Underground Railroad.

1850—The Compromise of 1850 includes a Fugitive Slave law requiring the return of escaped slaves.

1857—The *Dred Scott* decision of the U.S. Supreme Court declares that slaves are not U.S. citizens.

1861—The Confederate attack on Fort Sumter begins the Civil War.

1863—President Lincoln issues the Emancipation Proclamation.

1865—The Civil War ends; President Lincoln is assassinated.

   —The 13th Amendment officially ends slavery.

   —The Ku Klux Klan is organized in Tennessee to violently deny civil rights to African Americans.

1881—Booker T. Washington becomes the principal of Tuskegee Institute and presses African Americans to focus on economic success.

1896—George Washington Carver begins his long career as an inventor, scientist, and teacher at Tuskegee Institute.

1909—W. E. B. Du Bois and some African Americans from the Niagara Movement found the NAACP to fight for racial equality.

1914—World War I begins. Thousands of African Americans begin the long migration from the South to the Northern cities.

1917—Marcus Garvey brings the Universal Negro Improvement Association to Harlem.

1920s—The Harlem Renaissance, a literary movement, begins with the writing of Langston Hughes.

1920s—Louis Armstrong and Duke Ellington lead a jazz movement based on African American folk music called the blues.

1929—Martin Luther King Jr. is born.

1939—Marian Anderson sings at the Lincoln Memorial after she is refused the right to use Constitution Hall.

1940—Benjamin O. Davis Sr. becomes the first African American general in the U.S. Army.

1941—The U.S. enters World War II with more than one million African American troops in segregated units.

1947—Jackie Robinson breaks the color barrier in baseball.

Timeline of African American Events *(cont.)*

1954—The *Brown v. Board of Education* decision by the Supreme Court outlaws racial segregation in public schools.

1955—Rosa Parks refuses to give up her seat, sparking the Montgomery bus boycott led by Dr. King.

1957—The Southern Christian Leadership Council (SCLC) is formed.

—Nine African American students enroll in a Little Rock high school.

1960—The Student Nonviolent Coordinating Committee (SNCC) is formed using sit-ins to counteract discrimination in restaurants.

1961—The Congress of Racial Equality (CORE) begins freedom rides on interstate buses throughout the South.

1963—Dr. King delivers the "I Have a Dream" speech during the March on Washington to more than 250,000 marchers.

—Four young girls are killed in a church bombing in Birmingham.

1964—The 24th Amendment to the U.S. Constitution eliminates the poll tax, a fee for voting, in federal elections.

—The Civil Rights Act prohibits discrimination in public facilities and in jobs.

—Dr. King receives the Nobel Peace Prize for his nonviolent leadership.

1965—A peaceful protest movement in Selma, Alabama, leads to violence and national outrage over Selma police brutality.

—President Johnson signs the Voting Rights Act.

1965—The Watts riot in Los Angeles causes thirty-four deaths.

1967—Thurgood Marshall becomes the first African American Supreme Court justice.

1968—Dr. King is assassinated.

—President Johnson signs the second Civil Rights Act.

1991—General Colin Powell becomes the first African American Chairman of the Joint Chiefs of Staff.

1992—Carol Moseley Braun becomes the first African American woman elected to the U.S. Senate.

2001—Powell becomes the first African American Secretary of State.

2008—Barack Obama is elected as the first African American President.

Assignment

- Find at least ten dates in American history to add to the timeline. These dates could include wars, inventions, presidential elections, disasters, or sporting events, among many others.

- Create a visual timeline with these facts on a roll of white paper, such as shelf paper, rolled computer paper, or small adding-machine rolls.

- Block off squares or rectangles with a ruler.

- Write the date and the event at the top of the square.

- Draw a picture to illustrate each event in the lower half of each square. Use your books and other sources to help you.

- Use colored pencils or thin line markers to color each event.

African American Biographies

A biography tells the life of a person who did something significant in the world. There are many biographies written about the lives of African Americans who have influenced history.

Assignment

1. Read one biography about an important African American figure or a collective biography (see Annotated Bibliography on page 93) that features several people. Use the list on the next page or select another biography from the library that appeals to you.

2. List ten interesting events in the person's life. Use the discussion starters below to give you ideas for the important events. Share your list with a small group or the class.

Ten Important Events in the Subject's Life

1. _____
2. _____
3. _____
4. _____
5. _____
6. _____
7. _____
8. _____
9. _____
10. _____

Discussion Starters

1. What did the subject of the biography you read do that was important for him, her, or the country?
2. How did the experiences of the person's youth affect his or her adult life?
3. What experiences, events, people, or ideas led this person to oppose slavery, segregation, or discrimination?
4. What leadership qualities did the subject demonstrate?
5. Would you have liked to know this person? Why?
6. Describe how your subject displayed courage, loyalty, and honor.
7. What did your person accomplish in his or her life?
8. What was the greatest challenge your subject faced?
9. What was the saddest event in the life of the person?
10. What lessons can you learn about life from the person you read about?

Thinking About History

- How has the country changed since the lifetime of the person you read about?

- What progress still has to be made so that "all men are created equal" will be true in this country?

African American Biographies (cont.)

Bisson, Terry. *Nat Turner: Slave Revolt Leader.* Philadelphia, PA: Chelsea House, 1988.
This is a clear, easy-to read account of the famous slave revolt.

Bolden, Tonya. *George Washington Carver.* New York: Abrams Books for Young Readers, 2008.
This is an exceptional, short account of Carver's life.

Dray, Philip. *Yours for Justice, Ida B. Wells: The Daring Life of a Crusading Journalist.* Atlanta, GA: Peachtree, 2008.
This is a superb account of Wells's life in picture-book format for older readers.

Fradin, Dennis Brindell and Judith Bloom Frindell. *Ida B. Wells: Mother of the Civil Rights Movement.* New York: Clarion, 2000.
This is a very detailed account of the life of this extraordinary crusader.

Gaines, Ann. *Matthew Henson and the North Pole Expedition.* Chanhassen, MN: Child's World, 2000.
This is a very readable story of Henson's early life and his explorations.

Gentry, Tony. *Paul Laurence Dunbar.* Philadelphia, PA: Chelsea House, 1988.
This is an excellent account of the life and writing of one of the most famous 19th century African American poets.

Gregson, Susan R. *James Beckwourth: Mountaineer, Scout, and Pioneer.* Mankato, MN: Compass Point Books, 2006.
This is an enjoyable, detailed, very readable story of the scout's adventurous life.

Harper, Judith E. *Maya Angelou.* Chanhassen, MN: Child's World, 1999.
This is a clear account of the poet's life.

Johnson, Dolores. *Onward: A Photobiography of Polar Explorer Matthew Henson.* Washington, DC: National Geographic, 2005.
This is an excellent account of Henson's personal life and career as an explorer.

Landau, Elaine. *Bill Pickett: Wild West Cowboy.* Berkeley Heights, NJ: Enslow, 2004.
This is a brief, interesting biography of the life and adventures of cowboy and rodeo rider Bill Pickett.

Lowery, Linda. *Aunt Clara Brown: Official Pioneer.* Minneapolis, MN: Carolrhoda Books, 1999.
This is a superb story of one African American woman's success as a business woman and the long search for her daughter.

McDonough, Yona Zeldis. *Who Was Harriet Tubman?* Logan, IA: Perfection Learning, 2002.
This is an easy-to-read account of the life of the Underground Railroad conductor.

McLendon, Jacquelyn Y. *Phillis Wheatley: A Revolutionary Poet.* New York: Rosen, 2003.
This is a superior account of the poet's life and times.

Meadows, James. *Marian Anderson.* Chanhassen, MN: Child's World, 2001.
This is a clear, brief account of the singer's life.

Troy, Don. *W. E. B. Du Bois.* Chanhassen, MN: Child's World, 1999.
This is a brief but excellent account of Du Bois's life and accomplishments.

African American Heroes and Heroines

Ralph Abernathy—civil rights leader

Marian Anderson—voice for freedom

James Baldwin—author and critic of segregation

Benjamin Banneker—colonial scientist and inventor

Mary McLeod Bethune—founder of schools and a college

Ruby Bridges—went to an all-white school as a child

Henry Brown—mailed himself to freedom

Shirley Chisholm—educator and congresswoman

Samuel Cornish—started the first African American newspaper with John Russwurm

William and Ellen Craft—slaves who wore disguises in order to escape their owners

Benjamin O. Davis Jr.—Tuskegee airman and general

Elizabeth Eckford—one of the Little Rock Nine

Duke Ellington—great jazz musician

Marcus Garvey—moved the Universal Negro Improvement Association from Jamaica to Harlem to inspire African American pride

Eliza Harris—escape inspired Harriet Beecher Stowe

John Lewis—freedom rider and congressman

Reverend Jermain Wesley Loguen—abolitionist and bishop

Malcolm X—controversial opponent to nonviolent methods

Toni Morrison—Nobel Prize-winning author

Jessie Owens—Olympic runner

Bill Pickett—cowboy and rodeo star

Colin Powell—first African American Chairman of Joint Chiefs and Secretary of State

David Richmond—one of the Greensboro Four

Jackie Robinson—broke baseball's color barrier

Dred Scott—sued for freedom but lost

Fred Shuttlesworth—Alabama leader for civil rights

Sarah Walker—provided many jobs for women and donated money to combat lynching

Supporters

Lyndon B. Johnson—president who signed Voting Rights Act

John F. Kennedy—35th President of the United States

Eleanor Roosevelt—wife to President Theodore Roosevelt and passionate advocate for African American rights

Harriet Beecher Stowe—antislavery author of *Uncle Tom's Cabin*

Jim Zwerg—Freedom Rider

| 1500 | 1550 | 1600 | 1650 | 1700 | 1750 | 1800 | 1850 | 1900 | 1950 | 2000 |

Researching Events

Assignment

1. Research at least one event in African American history. Choose an event listed on this page or choose any other event that you know about.
2. Find information about your chosen event using the Important Information list below.
3. Take notes and then write a detailed paragraph.

Events in African American History

- The *La Amistad* revolt
- William and Ellen Craft "steal" themselves
- Henry "Box" Brown mails himself to freedom
- Frederick Douglass's escape
- Any of Harriet Tubman's escapes along the Underground Railroad
- Eliza Harris leaps across the ice to freedom
- Marian Anderson's efforts to sing at Constitution Hall
- Jackie Robinson joins the Dodgers
- The 1963 March on Washington
- The Birmingham demonstrations of 1963
- Rosa Parks refuses to give up her bus seat
- The Montgomery bus boycott
- Ruby Bridges goes to school
- The Woolworth lunch counter sit-ins
- The Little Rock Nine try to enter Central High
- *Brown v. Board of Education* (1954)
- James Meredith enters the University of Mississippi
- The March from Selma to Montgomery
- The Freedom Rides of 1961

Important Information About Your Chosen Event

- Date of the event
- Place of the event (state, city, town, etc.)
- Length of the event (in days)
- Important leaders involved in the actual event
- Numbers of people on each side
- Problems faced by African Americans
- Behavior of whites during the event
- Special acts of bravery during the event
- Results of the event (who won, effect on public morale, etc.)

African American Experiences

Assignment

1. Research one of the experiences in African American life listed below. Use the Internet, classroom sources, and books listed on the Annotated Bibliography and African American Biographies (pages 93 and 80).

2. Take careful notes about what you find in your research. List at least ten things that happened to an individual or group.

3. Write a detailed paragraph to share with the class.

Notes

1. _____
2. _____
3. _____
4. _____
5. _____
6. _____
7. _____
8. _____
9. _____
10. _____

Experiences in African American Life

- Treatment of a slave during the "Middle Passage" from Africa to America
- Life as a slave on a Southern plantation
- Life as a slave in the North
- Life as a free African American
- Life under black codes or Jim Crow laws
- Lynching and other unpunished murders
- A Ku Klux Klan attack
- Life as an African American soldier in the Civil War, the Indian wars, World War I, World War II, Korea Conflict, or Vietnam War
- Travel in the segregated South
- Violence or riots in cities
- Marching for civil rights
- "Whites only" and "Colored" accommodations
- Taking a Freedom Ride
- Trying to vote in the South from 1865 to 1965
- Getting a job in the South
- Getting an education in schools and colleges

Become a Famous Person

A great way to really understand African American history is to embody an important African American hero or heroine or a supporter, such as a Freedom Rider, civil rights marcher, political leader, or Underground Railroad leader. You will become familiar not only with the person, but also with the times in which he or she lived. You will understand the issues of the day and acquire a sense of the day-to-day lifestyle of your hero.

Do the Research

- Choose an African American figure or famous person from the list on page 81 or another person that you have learned about. Read enough about the individual to make sure that it is someone who really interests you.

- Use the research model below to find out everything you can about the person. Know the important dates, the vital statistics, the personal life, and the struggles of your character. Become familiar with your person's accomplishments. Begin to think of yourself as that person. Try to assume the attitude and the personality of your hero or heroine.

Go to the Sources

- Use biographies, the Internet, encyclopedias, almanacs, and other sources of information to acquire the basic facts you need.

- You should find and use at least two full-length biographies about your person.

- Use the index and table of contents of a biography to target specific information you need to know more about.

Take Careful Notes

- Rephrase the information in your own words.

- Write your facts clearly and briefly.

- Write down the basic facts in an orderly way. (The outline on page 86 is a good sample to use.)

- Look for anecdotes and funny stories about your person.

- Study the notes.

- Get a friend to quiz you about your person so that you know what you need to study and are confident about what you know.

- When other students are being questioned, write down questions you couldn't answer about your own character, and look the answers up later.

Become a Famous Person *(cont.)*

Be Famous

"My name is _____. What would you like to know about me?"

This is one way to begin your presentation. You might also want to give a brief presentation, listing five or six important facts about your famous person. This will give your classmates a place to begin with their questions. Have a story to tell or something else interesting to say if there is a momentary lull in the questioning.

Stay in Character

Don't forget who you are. You are a famous person, not another student in the class. Be very serious. Avoid any silly behaviors. At the end of the questions, review the important facts about your life.

Be Dramatic

- Use a loud voice. Don't drop your voice at the end of sentences.
- Use gestures. Use your arms to emphasize your points.
- Take charge of the classroom. Stride across the front.
- Be forceful, assertive, and self-assured. Have faith in yourself.

Get in Costume

- Put together an appropriate costume. Check your closets at home for pants, shirts, or old costumes that might work. Check with parents, grandparents, older siblings, and friends for articles of clothing that might help. Ask for help getting to thrift stores for the missing pieces.
- Dark gray, blue, or black athletic pants can often serve as the trousers.

Reminders for Doing Reports

- Use as many sources as possible, including textbooks, encyclopedias, Internet Web sites, and books about African Americans.
- Take notes carefully.
- Use your own words. Don't copy sentences.
- Don't use complete sentences in notes.
- Get all of the facts.
- Arrange the notes in order by time and place.

Become a Famous Person *(cont.)*

Directions: Use these guidelines to help you find important information about your famous person. See page 81 for a list of famous people.

Research Guidelines

I. Youth

   A. Birthplace and date

   B. Home life and experiences

      1. Siblings (brothers and sisters)

      2. Places lived (parts of the country; farm or town)

      3. Circumstances (rich or poor)

   C. Schooling (When? How much?)

   D. Childhood heroes

   E. Interesting facts and stories about your youth

II. Personal Experiences

   A. Experiences in life

      1. Your position in society (slave, civil rights worker, writer, founder of an organization, etc.)

      2. Troubles you faced (Give details of your actions.)

   B. Lifestyle and personal habits

      1. Personal attitude toward life (List examples.)

      2. Values you believe in

   C. Reasons for fame

      1. Accomplishments (Name and describe successes.)

      2. Failures and things you didn't complete

III. End of Life

   A. Death

      1. Date of death and age at time of death

      2. Cause of death (facts about the death)

   B. Fame

      1. Were you famous at the time of death?

      2. Were you admired or forgotten by the time of your death?

IV. The Life and Times

   A. Contemporaries

      1. Other people you met

      2. Presidents and public leaders of the time

   B. Inventions and discoveries

      1. Important inventions of the time period

      2. Discoveries in medicine, science, or exploration

   C. Travel and transportation

      1. How people traveled (boats, horses, other means)

      2. How goods and products were moved

Barack Obama

Barack Obama was born on August 4, 1961, in Hawaii. His parents were Ann Dunham, a white woman from Kansas, and Barack Obama Sr., a graduate of Harvard University, who was born on a farm in Kenya. His parents met at a college in Hawaii. His mother later divorced Barack's father and married an Indonesian named Lolo Soetoro. Barack lived in Djakarta, Indonesia, and attended school there. He learned the Indonesian language.

In 1971, Obama returned to Hawaii to live with his grandparents with whom he grew very close. He entered Occidental College in Los Angeles at the age of eighteen and, two years later, transferred to Columbia University, where he graduated in 1983 with a degree in political science. In the following three years, Barack worked as a community organizer in poor areas of Chicago, visited Kenya where his father had died in 1982, and entered Harvard Law School. In 1990, he became the first African American editor of the prestigious *Harvard Law Review*.

In 1991, he graduated from Harvard with honors and became a civil rights attorney in Chicago the next year. He married Michelle Robinson, an attorney and hospital administrator, in 1992 at Trinity Church. In 1995, his memoir entitled *Dreams from My Father: A Story of Race and Inheritance* was published and was widely read. His mother soon died of cancer. In 1996, Barack was elected to the Illinois State Senate where he served for seven years. His first daughter, Malia, was born in 1998, and his second daughter, Natasha (Sasha), was born in 2001.

Obama was defeated in a primary race for Congress in 2000. In 2004, he was elected to the United States Senate from Illinois and gave a well-received speech to the Democratic National Convention

during prime time that gave him a national audience. In 2006, his second book, *The Audacity of Hope: Thoughts on Reclaiming the American Dream,* became a bestseller. On February 10, 2007, Barack Obama declared his candidacy for the Presidency of the United States. In 2008, he won a closely contested primary fight against Senator Hillary Clinton and became the Democratic nominee for president.

On November 4, 2008, Barack Obama was elected the 44th president of the United States with 53% of the popular vote and 365 electoral votes. He immediately faced a huge economic crisis, greater than anything since the Great Depression. His negotiating skills and ability to get people to work together was tested as he faced many crises, including two wars in the Middle East, a worldwide economic crisis, and many domestic challenges, such as healthcare and education in America.

Know Your Government

It is important to know who your elected representatives are and where they stand on important issues.

Assignment

1. Use the Internet, almanacs, and other sources to find the name and party affiliation of each of the elected positions listed.

2. Find one issue that is important to you that they have supported or opposed. The issues might have to do with school funding, healthcare for children, driving rules, or war and peace.

Federal Government

President of the United States: _____

Party: _____

Issue: _____

United States Senator (1): _____

Party: _____

Issue: _____

United States Senator (2): _____

Party: _____

Issue: _____

Congressperson (House of Representatives): _____

Party: _____

Issue: _____

State Government

State: _____

Governor: _____

Party: _____

Issue: _____

State Senator: _____

Party: _____

Issue: _____

Assemblyperson (State Assembly): _____

Party: _____

Issue: _____

Local Government

Mayor: _____

City Council Members: _____

_____

Issue: _____

1500, 1550, 1600, 1650, 1700, 1750, 1800, 1850, 1900, 1950, 2000

1500   1550   1600   1650   1700   1750   1800   1850   1900   1950   2000

The Law Matters

The civil rights movement was successful in large part because the courts, especially the Supreme Court, determined the ultimate law of the land in cases such as school desegregation, voting rights, and equal access to public facilities, such as buses, lunch counters, and restrooms.

Directions: Use the Internet, almanacs, and other resources to name the nine justices of the United States Supreme Court. List one fact about each justice.

Chief Justice: _____

Fact: _____

Justice: _____

Fact: _____

Justice: _____

Fact: _____

Justice: _____

Fact: _____

Justice: _____

Fact: _____

Justice: _____

Fact: _____

Justice: _____

Fact: _____

Justice: _____

Fact: _____

Justice: _____

Fact: _____

Supreme Court Decisions

Directions: Name two Supreme Court decisions from the present or past, and tell what the decision meant as shown in the sample.

    Example: Decision: *Brown v. Board of Education*
            Meaning: Schools may not be segregated. Separate is not equal.

  1. Decision: _____

      Meaning: _____

  2. Decision: _____

      Meaning: _____

1500 1550 1600 1650 1700 1750 1800 1850 1900 1950 2000

Collecting Oral Histories

Older Americans lived through the events of the civil rights movement. Some were directly involved in the effort to achieve civil rights, and others were witnesses who lived through the events or watched them on television as they happened.

Directions: Interview an older relative, friend, or neighbor who was a witness to the civil rights movement. Use this form as a guide for questioning.

Name: _____

Place(s) you were living during the 1950s and 1960s

_____

What you were doing (studying, working, serving in the military, etc.)

_____

Images you remember from television or personal involvement

_____

_____

_____

Special personal memories of events

_____

_____

_____

People you knew who were involved and what they did

_____

_____

_____

Your personal feelings about the entire period or specific events

_____

_____

_____

People you especially admired from the time and your reasons for admiration

_____

_____

_____

Final reflections on the movement

_____

_____

_____

| 1500 | 1550 | 1600 | 1650 | 1700 | 1750 | 1800 | 1850 | 1900 | 1950 | 2000 |

Celebrate African American History Day

Set aside one day to be devoted to activities related to your study of African Americans. You might call it African American History Day and possibly coordinate it with African American History Month in February. If possible, do this activity with two or three classes at the same grade level. This allows you to share some of the group tasks and provides a special experience for the entire grade level. The activities suggested can revisit some of the classroom experiences you have already had and will serve as a review.

Costumes—Famous Persons

Encourage each of your students to come dressed in costume as the famous African American or supporter that he or she portrayed in the famous person research project.

Parent Help

Encourage as many parents or older siblings as you can to come for all or part of the day to enjoy the proceedings and to help set up and monitor the activities. This is truly a day to involve the family in the educational process. It helps to survey parents for any special talents, interests, or hobbies that would be a match for specific centers.

Doing Centers

- The centers you set up should relate in some way to the history of African Americans.
- Centers should involve the children doing an activity and often making, writing, or illustrating something they can take or put on display.
- The class should be divided into groups with about five to seven students in each group.
- Each center should take about fifteen to twenty minutes. Students then rotate to the next activity.
- The following suggestions will get you started. You will want to add any others for which you have a special expertise.

Eat Heartily

If you have parent volunteers, plan a potluck luncheon with a civil rights rally or a similar theme. Parents and students could do the decorations together at one of the centers.

Rally Posters and Poems

Use large pieces of tagboard or construction paper and bold markers to make posters promoting one or several civil rights activities, such as a sit-in, boycott, Freedom Ride, march, or voter registration drive.

Students can work in pairs and practice their paired poetry using the songs in this book or poems by featured poets, such as Langston Hughes.

Celebrate African American History Day *(cont.)*

Oral History

Have students in each group read their oral history reports that they completed with older adults who remembered the civil rights movement. Have students share and discuss their reflections on these reports.

Quiz Show

Have students write questions (with answers) to be asked to individual students or teams in a quiz show format like *Jeopardy*. The questions could be done ahead of time and given to a parent master-of-ceremonies.

Dancing

The dance center could feature popular music and dances from the civil rights period. An older volunteer could show students the dance moves.

Sports Skills

African Americans have been very successful in professional sports whenever they have been allowed to compete. Use this center on the playground to do simple skills in baseball, football, and basketball. Playing catch, shooting baskets, and doing similar activities would be good. Get a volunteer parent sports fan to supervise this center.

Readers' Theater

The readers' theater center involves practicing with a script for a readers' theater presentation. The script could be the one in this book or one that children have written. Children at this center could also collaboratively write and perform a script.

Creative Arts Center

Students at this center could recreate portraits of famous African Americans with colored pencils (or just pencils). Modeling or sculpting clay could be available for students to do miniature busts of famous African Americans. Those interested in literature could compose songs, speeches, or poems with an African American theme.

Read a Book

Students sometimes appreciate a quiet reading center as an activity break. Books with African American themes could be available to read. This would allow children a quiet period between more active centers.

Annotated Bibliography

Collective Biographies

Adler, David A. *Heroes for Civil Rights*. New York: Holiday House, 2007.
    This includes brief accounts of the lives of African Americans who led the modern civil rights movement.

Colman, Penny. *Adventurous Women: Eight True Stores About Women Who Made a Difference*. New York: Holt, 2006.
    This includes excellent accounts of the work of Alice Hamilton, Mary McLeod Bethune, and Biddy Mason.

Fradin, Dennis Brindell. *Bound for the North Star: True Stories of Fugitive Slaves*. New York: Clarion, 2000.
    This includes exciting accounts of slaves who escaped to freedom.

Garrison, Mary. *Slaves Who Dared: The Stories of Ten African American Heroes*. Shippensburg, PA: White Mane, 2002.
    This contains great stories of bravery and persistence by slaves who fought for their freedom.

Hudson, Wade. *Great Black Heroes: Five Brave Explorers*. New York: Cartwheel, 1995.
    This briefly introduces the accomplishments of five African American explorers.

Wilkinson, Brenda. *African American Women Writers*. Hoboken, NJ: Wiley, 1999.
    This is a good account of poets and writers from Phillis Wheatley to Alice Walker.

History of the Civil Rights Movement

Bausum, Ann. *Freedom Riders: John Lewis and Jim Zwerg on the Front Lines of the Civil Rights Movement*. Washington, DC: National Geographic, 2005.
    This is a readable account of the efforts of the freedom riders.

Landau, Elaine. *The Civil Rights Movement in America*. Danbury, CT: Children's Press, 2007.
    This is a clear, concise history of the movement.

McWhorter, Diane. *A Dream of Freedom: The Civil Rights Movement from 1954 to 1968*. New York: Scholastic, 2004.
    This is a complete and well-written account of the movement from the *Brown* decision to the death of Dr. King.

Rappaport, Doreen. *Nobody Gonna Turn Me 'Round: Stories and Songs of the Civil Rights Movement*. Somerville, MA: Candlewick, 2006.
    This includes vignettes from the lives of ordinary and famous African Americans who took a stand for civil rights.

Stovall, TaRessa. *Buffalo Soldiers*. St. Louis, MO: San Val, 1999.
    This is an enjoyable account of the black troops of the frontier.

Turck, Mary C. *Freedom Song: Young Voices and the Struggle for Civil Rights*. Chicago, IL: Chicago Review Press, 2008.
    This is an outstanding account of the part that songs played in the civil rights movement during the 1950s and 1960s and the songs themselves.

Venable, Rose. *The Civil Rights Movement*. Mankato, MN: Child's World, 2002.
    This includes a brief overview of the basic events in the movement.

Glossary

abolitionist—a person opposed to slavery

activist—a person who works hard and takes risks for his or her beliefs

assassination—murder for political reasons

autobiography—the story of a person's life told by him- or herself

biography—the story of a person's life

bondage—slavery

boycott—to refuse to buy or use something as a protest

civil rights—a person's rights to freedom and equality

conductor—a person who led fugitive slaves from one safe place to another

CORE—Congress of Racial Equality

demonstrations—public protests, usually with speakers

desegregation—ending the segregation of people by race

discrimination—unfair treatment to people because they are different

emancipate—to give liberty to slaves

federal—relating to the national government, not the states

Freedom Rides—trips taken on buses or trains through the South to end segregation

fugitive—a person on the run from the law

integrate—to make public places open to all races

interstate transportation—buses and trains that cross state lines

Jim Crow laws—laws passed in the South to keep races separated

legislature—a place where representatives make laws

lynching—to put to death illegally by hanging

NAACP—National Association for the Advancement of Colored People

nonviolent resistance—a tactic in which protesters do not strike back

overseer—a white man paid to keep slaves working and obedient

plantation—a large farm usually with one or two cash crops

revolution—a fight against a system of government

SCLC—Southern Christian Leadership Conference

segregation—separation of people by race

sit-in—protest used to occupy segregated lunch counters

SNCC—Student Nonviolent Coordinating Committee

unconstitutional—not legal under the U.S. Constitution

Underground Railroad—a system of people and hiding places to help fugitive slaves

Answer Key

Page 36

1.	c	6.	b
2.	c	7.	b
3.	b	8.	d
4.	d	9.	b
5.	a	10.	d

Page 37

1.	d	6.	c
2.	c	7.	a
3.	b	8.	b
4.	a	9.	c
5.	c	10.	c

Page 38

1.	b	6.	d
2.	a	7.	b
3.	b	8.	d
4.	b	9.	a
5.	a	10.	c

Page 39

1.	a	6.	a
2.	a	7.	d
3.	a	8.	d
4.	c	9.	d
5.	c	10.	a

Page 40

1.	c	6.	d
2.	d	7.	d
3.	d	8.	b
4.	c	9.	a
5.	b	10.	d

Page 41

1.	b	6.	d
2.	b	7.	c
3.	d	8.	c
4.	b	9.	d
5.	c	10.	d

Page 42

1.	d	6.	c
2.	a	7.	c
3.	c	8.	a
4.	d	9.	c
5.	c	10.	d

Page 63
Discussion Starters

1. His brother is in the sixth grade, and he may get picked on or bothered by Byron and other sixth-grade boys who don't like him "showing them up."

2. The boys are very poor, have few clothes to wear, and do not have much to eat. They come from Arkansas, and their "country" speech patterns are different.

3. Kenny's mom sends extra food to share with the boys, and she helps them become friends again after Kenny hurts Rufus's feelings.

4. Answers will vary.

5. He defends Kenny against other bullies, recovers his stolen gloves, and comforts him after the bombing when they return home.

6. He's worried that his sister has been killed and later retreats into himself in reaction to what he sees in the bombed church.

7. She seems less strict and less "proper" to Mrs. Watson.

8. They took food because they couldn't stop easily at restaurants or find places that served African Americans. They also prepared for sleeping in the car and stopping for restroom needs in parks where they were allowed.

Page 64
Discussion Starters

1. Answers will vary.

2. They know that he is probably an orphan and surely homeless and want to make sure he has some food.

3. Bud and the other Hooverville residents are usually chased away or hassled by police because the nearby towns had so little money to support or feed the poor.

4. Three examples of kindness: the family who pretends Bud is their child in the breakfast line, the families who share with him at the Hooverville, and Lefty Lewis who helps him find his grandfather.

5. Answers will vary.

6. Most students will be opposed to the destruction of the Hooverville because the poor had no place to go, and they did not appear to cause any trouble. However, they were seen as an embarrassment to the town by some townspeople.

7. Answers will vary.

8. He probably doesn't want to be reminded of the long-ago conflict with Bud's mother or her death.

9. Answers will vary.

10. He quickly learns to play the recorder and the sax.

11. Herman is Bud's grandfather.

12. They argue, and Bud's mother leaves home.

Answer Key *(cont.)*

Page 65

Discussion Starters

1. Elijah is determined, very personable, easygoing, sometimes inclined to act before thinking, and very well meaning toward others. He is easily embarrassed and proud of his family and race.

2. Elijah is skilled at throwing rocks, a good caregiver for animals, an excellent rider, and good with tools.

3. Elijah helps a new family arriving from the South, works hard for Mr. Leroy, and helps Mrs. Holton and the chained-up slaves as best as he can.

4. Sometimes the preacher shows courage and determination. Other times, he is an untrustworthy character with very poor judgment. The preacher lies to many people, including Elijah. He also steals Mr. Leroy's money—money intended to free Mr. Leroy's family. Then the preacher gambles this money away.

5. Some embarrassing things include grabbing a snake out of a jar, throwing up on Frederick Douglass as an infant, misunderstanding Mr. Travis's lesson on manners, and using an improper word with Mr. Leroy.

6. He takes the baby to his family when the chained slave mother asks him to.

7. Answers will vary.

Understanding Character and Theme

- Elijah's understanding of the world, the evils and conflicts of slavery, and the value of human life and freedom grow. He becomes serious and responsible in tracking down the preacher, accepting what he can do to save one child, and representing himself and his people honorably. His parents, Mr. Leroy, and his teachers all helped in various ways.

- The most profound theme is probably the value of human life and liberty. Others include the savagery and evil effects of human slavery on slaves and slave-owners and that most people have varying amounts of good and evil in their character.

- Other themes include the value of schooling, the importance of family, the universality of love, the impact of history for good and evil purposes, the need for all to accept personal responsibility, and the wonderful and fruitful nature of friendship at many ages and levels.

Page 74

Free States (white)

1. Maine
2. New Hampshire
3. Vermont
4. Massachusetts
5. Connecticut
6. Rhode Island
7. New York
8. New Jersey
9. Pennsylvania
10. Ohio
11. Indiana
12. Illinois
13. Iowa
14. Michigan
15. Wisconsin
16. California

Slave States (gray)

1. Delaware
2. Maryland
3. Virginia
4. Kentucky
5. Missouri
6. Texas
7. Arkansas
8. Tennessee
9. North Carolina
10. South Carolina
11. Georgia
12. Florida
13. Alabama
14. Mississippi
15. Louisiana

Page 75

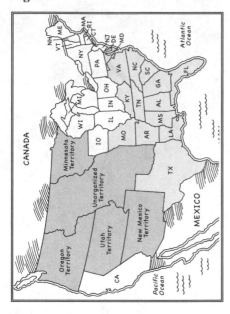

Page 76

1. California
2. New York
3. Kansas
4. Mississippi
5. Alabama
6. Arkansas
7. North Carolina
8. Washington, D.C.
9. Virginia
10. Massachusetts

Page 88

Answers will vary depending on the year.

Page 89

As of 2011:

Chief Justice: John G. Roberts Jr.

Justices: Samuel Anthony Alito Jr., Stephen G. Breyer, Ruth Bader Ginsburg, Elena Kagan, Anthony M. Kennedy, Antonin Scalia, Sonia Sotomayor, and Clarence Thomas

Facts will vary.

Supreme Court decisions will vary.